The Bloody Experience's Hell Reeducation Camp

The Bloody Experience's Hell Reeducation Camp

The Inhuman Treatment of Vietnamese Prisoners of War

Quang Hong Mac
(Raphael M.V. Mac)

Strategic Book Publishing and Rights Co.

Strategic Book Publishing & Rights Co., LLC
USA | Singapore
www.sbpra.net

For information about special discounts for bulk purchases, please contact Strategic Book Publishing and Rights Co. Special Sales, at bookorder@sbpra.net.

ISBN: 978-1-952269-08-0

This book is dedicated to my deceased parents and Mac ancestors.

Acknowledgments

I thank the members of the Mac lineage and all my friends who encouraged my writing for the third book without my wife, Nguyễn Ngọc Hoa, who was a tireless supporter.

I also leave the knowledge and the radicalness of the Mac lineage to my sons Mạc Hồng Đức and Mạc Hồng Trí, and to my daughters Mạc Ngọc Lan Anh and Mạc Ngọc Lan Chi.

A special acknowledgment to my grandchildren, Mạc Hiều Andy, Mạc P. Chianna, Âu M. T. Natalia, Âu M.T. Nathan, and a welcome our new granddaughter Phou Mac Diễm.

Table of Contents

Foreword

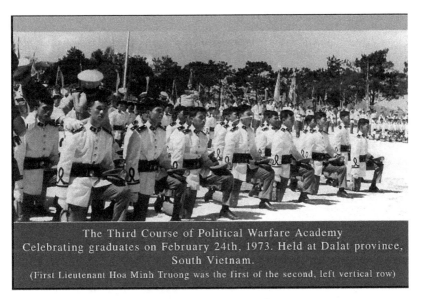

The Third Course of Political Warfare Academy
Celebrating graduates on February 24th, 1973. Held at Dalat province,
South Vietnam.
(First Lieutenant Hoa Minh Truong was the first of the second, left vertical row)

The class of the Political Warfare Academy graduated
on February 24, 1973, at Dalat Province, South Viet Nam.
(First Lieutenant Hoa Minh Truong is
the first on the left in the second row.)

Western Australia
December 17, 2019

Karl Marx is the elite's most dishonest academic. While jobless
and stateless after being forced to leave his native Germany due
to his political views, he avenged the hardship by writing books

that instructed governments on how to rob, kill, and enslave their people. And his dishonest character didn't discriminate against his main supporter, Friedrich Engels, who descended from a long line of capitalists. Capitalists were Marx's enemies. The people condemned Engels as a traitor. How could the leftist follow and adore Karl Marx?

When an honest person suffers such difficulties as Marx, they try to work to improve their condition. A dishonest person solves the hardship by robbery and fraud. Karl Marx represents the master of the dishonest line, but he was lucky enough to live in a generous country like Great Britain, where he was allowed to express himself freely, unlike places like France, where he was often harassed by the authorities. The Communist League held its second congress in London from November 29 to December 8 of 1847, and there Marx and Engels were tasked with writing the first manifesto for the Communist Party.

Marx tried to destroy human history and human society with his crazy ideas. He acted as God, explaining that humans descended from apes. Indeed, no one can explain and confirm the exact origin of man. Most religions believe man was created by God, not descended from a monkey. Unfortunately, Marx's followers are so proud to be the descendants of apes that they lose their human minds. Communists act with animal instincts. They have waged genocide labeled as revolution.

Starting in October 1917, Lenin transformed Marx's foolish theory into reality in Russia, and communism has spread globally, including in democratic places like the US, Europe, and Australia. Communism has become disastrous for humanity. It has been responsible for killing more than one hundred million people and enslaving a billion more. Moreover, democratic countries, including those in the West, are facing many complications brought on by people who believe in communism.

Atheism spread worldwide. The dishonest component favored Marx's handbook in committing serious crimes and prospering on other people's sweat. Communism pulled human history back to the monarchic era, which promotes the idea that the king represents God in ruling the people.

Nowadays, Communists acclaim themselves as revolutionaries in dominating a country. The Reds (Communists) apply demagogic and terroristic policy to their people, all disguised behind propaganda. Totalitarian regimes are of the same character, but the Communists are far more dangerous and cruel than dynasties in the days of yore. The Communist cheats the people and hides behind nice language. Communist countries are labeled as a "paradise." Slave labor is called "glorious." Even the hell of prison is called "reeducation." Genocide is labeled as revolution, the class struggle, or social reform. There's an old saying: "When a Communist is born, a midwife sees the mouth."

The evil theories of Marxism-Leninism were renamed Maoism in China. When the idea of communism spread to Viet Nam under Ho Chi Minh, it was disastrous for humanity.

Marxism-Leninism has intoxicated the world since the first manifesto was released. Marx had declared war on humanity, on human history. He showed his hatred toward religion by saying: "Religion is the opium of the people." Indeed, Marxism is the drug of the people. Communism has poisoned people's minds. Innocent people, the ebullient young, inexpert academics, and the dishonest element have exploited Marxism to make money and collect power.

People identify drugs in multiple forms—opium, heroin, cocaine, crystal meth, and marijuana, but they also include cigarettes and alcohol. Addiction to drugs results in crime, social mayhem, social damage, and health problems. Both innocents and dishonest people become robot-humans after Marxism-

Leninism affects their minds, and they act without conscience. Marxist-Leninist pupils represented the Communist Party in controlling nations and killing its people in places like Viet Nam, China, Cuba, and other communist countries.

In the West, the victims of Marxism use the propaganda of the left-wing media and political parties to rebel, so society often faces protest, resulting in violence and division. The left-leaning parties formulate the three *D's*: deception, demagoguery, and destruction, and the left-wing media formulate the three *F's*: false polls, fake news, and fabricated stories. These common formulas have been applied in both communist states and democratic countries.

The Marxist-Leninist's drug can be easily recognized in communist parties, communist countries, among leftists, and the left-wing media. While drugs harm a person's health, the harm done by these principles to a person's mind is as dangerous as any drug. Drug trafficking is organized by cartels and syndicates. The Marxist-Leninist "drug" cartel in the Soviet Union and Eastern European Bloc countries collapsed in the early 1990s. As a result, the Maoists are currently the largest cartel of Marxism on the planet.

The common tactics of Communists have not changed; they repeat and cheat the innocent people, including the naïve politicians in the West. Examples of this include:

1. Talking During Fighting

During the Viet Nam War, the Vietcong and its master, China, plus the Soviet Union, engaged in peace talks with the US and the South Vietnamese government in Paris after the Tet Offensive in 1968. The Paris Peace Accords were eventually signed on January 27, 1973. It was a farce, but US Secretary of State Henry Kissinger and the prominent Vietcong terrorist, Lê Đức Thọ, were both awarded the Nobel Peace Prize in 1973.

Just as they had after the Geneva Conference agreement, signed on July 20, 1954, the North Viet Nam communists invaded South Viet Nam after the Paris Peace Accords and occupied Saigon on April 30, 1975.

Nowadays, China has recycled the talking during the trade fight with the US. The author of *The Art of the Deal* quickly learned about China's deception in its tariffs during the economic war.

2. Stalling
The Communists constantly bide their time while engaged in the low tide of revolution.

3. Taking One Step Back to Prepare for Three Steps Forward
The Communists never give up the fight. Their obstinate character never changes. The Communist just pretends to deal when facing weakness.

4. The Lizard Changes its Skin Color
After the Soviet Union collapsed in the early 1990s, for survival reasons, China and Viet Nam applied this tactic to cheat Western and democratic countries by saying that "the free market is led by socialism."

Communists are social dregs. They use people as if throwing away a lemon after the juice has been squeezed out. There's an old saying: "When a hunter recognizes its dog cannot do the job properly, a hunter must know how to eat the dog's meat."

Betrayal is a common tactic for Communists. The Communist trusts no one, including their close comrades. Do not trust communist talk! Watch what the Communists have done. The Communist represents traitors and deception. However, communism cannot cheat the world with its cunning tactics. The real face of the evil Communist has been exposed; the crimes against humanity couldn't be concealed forever.

The Communist ignores human life. Therefore, they always attach the word "people" into major titles. China named its regime the People's Republic of China, the People's Liberation Army, the People's Government of China. The Vietcong called their troops the People's Army of Viet Nam. North Korea is called the Democratic People's Republic of Korea, and its military the Korean People's Army.

The Communist character is ruthless. They have killed people without pity, starting with Lenin during the Bolshevik Revolution in October 1917. Communism has become the largest humanitarian disaster on the planet. The tactic of using human waves during the Korean War, espoused by Chairman Mao Tse Tung, proved that military genocide occurred in its communist army. Mao **sacrified a million troops** during the battle for Điện Biên Phủ. An untrained four-star general, Võ Nguyên Giáp, applied the human wave tactic against ten thousand entrenched French soldiers that resulted **a thousand Vietcong casualties**. Moreover, in the Viet Nam War, Hồ Chí Minh, Võ Nguyên Giáp, and Four-Star General Văn Tiến Dũng lost more than 1.5 million Vietcong troops, with nearly 300,000 missing, by the time the invasion concluded on April 30, 1975.

During war, Communists waste lives in exchange for a bloody victory, while democratic countries always respect the lives of their soldiers. The Vietcong exploited the humanity of the US and South Viet Nam to carry out psychological warfare when its soldiers were killed in battles, and the left-wing media propagated that to the West.

During the Tet Offensive in 1968, the Vietcong faced disaster. Hanoi lost more than 100,000 troops, but the left-wing media concealed that. Instead, propaganda misled the American people. The psychological warfare trap of the global communist bloc succeeded, affecting the minds of innocent people, and the leftist parties activated, sparking violent protests opposing the Viet Nam War while the soldiers of the US and South Viet Nam's Army of the Republic of Viet Nam (ARVN) were fighting against Vietcong terrorists. The Viet Nam War's protesters were innocent traitors, but the left-wing media committed treason.

The vulnerability of the Communists is the economy. Unfortunately, Europe, along with US presidents Bill Clinton, George W. Bush, and Barrack Obama, strengthened China's advantageous trade position. In fact, Bill Clinton's designation of China as a most favored nation (MFN) helped it grow even faster. The US, Europe, Australia, and other democratic countries have fallen into China's trade trap, government trap, and debt trap started many decades ago.

Nowadays, China's growth is the most serious threat on the planet, a dire consequence being paid after a critical mistake. The West fed the totalitarian regime's economy, strengthened its financial system, and promoted China in joining the World Trade Organization (WTO). China has exploited naïve national leaders, innocent politicians, and profit lovers' businesses to carry out its global hegemonic strategy.

China developed and made a huge profit from the West's loss, and stolen technology transformed the largest communist regime to a Red capitalist. Therefore, communism has never changed. The tiger snake has never become a python, and Satan cannot become an angel. The West has enriched China's economy, but that has not changed the communist regime. Instead, it created an opportunity for the world's most dangerous power to threaten everyone.

China's communist regime doesn't care about the people of Hong Kong. The people who live in the former British colony acquired a financial weapon, so China faltered when massive protests broke out in early June of 2019. China did not want a repeat of the Tiananmen Square incident in Hong Kong.

President Donald Trump struck at China's vulnerability. The tariffs made China flinch after its retaliatory tariffs on US agricultural products proved to be in vain. Instead, China's tariffs hit back at its own people on the mainland, fulfilling a saying: The sword made by China stabs the Chinese.

It was the reason China rushed into negotiations with the US. China reduced its brazen attitude after the economic woes and the potential crippling of its financial system, but Beijing silently applied malicious tactics to cheat the US in the deal. Mass joblessness was a risk for the regime. China applied the lessons of dynasties that collapsed in the old days that should repeat anytime, actually when the economy was ruined by the trade war.

Do not fear what the Communist does. Let's do what the Communist fears.

Mao Tse Tung killed many comrades and imprisoned Deng Xiaoping and Xi Zhongxun (father of Xi Jinping) in the Cultural Revolution after using Nguyễn Văn Trỗi in a terrorist mission to kill US Secretary of Defense Robert McNamara and Ambassador Henry Cabot Lodge in 1964. Nguyễn Văn Trỗi was sentenced to death. His wife, Quyên, just married a month, followed Vietcong undercover activists into the jungle. She was used like a sex slave in the Woman's Comfort Unit. She served high-ranking Communist Nguyễn Hữu Thọ, Mai Chí Thọ, and was sent to Hanoi to serve Ho Chi Minh. When beloved comrade Fidel Castro was needed, it was arranged for Quyên to travel to Cuba, where she served Castro for six months.

Lawyer Trịnh Đình Thảo was the actual henchman of the North Viet Nam Communists. After the Vietcong claimed the improbable victory on April 30, 1975, the Vietcong detained Trịnh Đình Thảo and his wife at their mansion in Saigon. The regime cut off water and food, and eventually Thảo and his wife died from starvation.

After the Vietcong breached the Paris Peace Accords, signed on January 27, 1973, North Viet Nam's communist government carried out the "dried bloodbath" policy as revenge against South Viet Nam. The ruthless regime threw more than 800,000 soldiers and public servants of South Viet Nam into its hell of a prison system. The Vietcong called it reeducation. The "reeducation" camps of the Vietcong were like Nazi Germany's concentration camps in the Second World War. The Vietcong badly treated South Vietnamese prisoners. The housing was abysmal, and the prisoners constantly faced starvation. The prisoners were tortured and executed, and sick people were not given access to medication. Add in spiritual intimidation and brainwashing, and the Vietcong killed more than 165,000 of those prisoners.

Unfortunately, the human rights agencies seemed asleep on this issue after the Viet Nam War ended on April 30, 1975. The leftist media and prominent Vietcong supporters in the West, like Jane Fonda, John Kerry, Joe Biden, and Bill and Hillary Clinton, have kept quiet as a stone. They have slept on the treason and the abuse of human rights.

Many victims of the Vietcong, soldiers and public servants, survived after spending time in the hell of the reeducation camps. Therefore, the bloody experiences levied by the communists have not been forgotten. Quang Hong Mac's book, *The Bloody Experiences in Hell's Reeducation Camp: The Inhumane Treatment of Vietnamese Prisoners of War,* shows a tiny scene inside the reeducation camps, but the crimes of the Vietcong are plenty.

I am so proud to write this introduction to the book. I believe readers will find the untold stories about the Viet Nam War and the Vietcong's hellish prison system horrifying. Finally, I congratulate Quang Hong Mac on publishing his new book, and I wish him good luck and best wishes.

Hoa Minh Truong,

Author of five books, founder and editor of thedawnmedia.com

INTRODUCTION I

John J. Gaittens, Philadelphia Deputy Police Commissioner (Ret.),
Currently CEO of Law Enforcement Health Benefits, Inc.

Mr. Quang Hong Mac is one of the most honorable, selfless, compassionate, and dedicated men I have ever had the pleasure of knowing. It is even more gratifying to call him my friend.

Upon meeting Mr. Mac, people are invariably struck by his humility and deference to others. Additionally, it is readily apparent that he is a man of great character and compassion.

It is not surprising in light of the fact that he is descended from the Mạc dynasty, which dates back to 770 BC and ruled in Viet Nam for over 150 years. The dynasty's influence extended into China and Korea as well.

Mạc Hồng Quang (known to Americans as Quang Hong Mac) was born in Vĩnh Long province on February 5, 1941. He proudly served as a captain in the South Vietnamese Army (ARVN) and was highly decorated for his courageous actions during the war, earning Bronze, Silver, and Gold Stars. Additionally, Captain Mac received the Purple Heart for injuries sustained in combat on May 5, 1968.

After the fall of Saigon on April 30, 1975, Quang Mac and thousands of other innocent South Vietnamese citizens were imprisoned in "reeducation" camps established by the new North Vietnamese-influenced government. After surviving five years of brutal treatment in the camps, he escaped and found it necessary to leave his homeland to come to the US by way of Malaysia.

While living in Pennsylvania, Mr. Mac studied and worked tirelessly to create a new life for himself and his family. However, Quang Mac's efforts were not solely focused on improving life for his family; he was also determined to improve conditions and opportunities for less fortunate immigrants. He volunteered to work with the people in the Vietnamese community in Philadelphia as a human rights advocate.

It was in this capacity that I met Mr. Mac. In 1994, Quang Mac volunteered his time to teach Philadelphia police officers how to speak and understand the Vietnamese language. There is a large Vietnamese community in Philadelphia, and unfortunately, due to their experience with law enforcement in their homeland, they are naturally distrustful and afraid of the police. Mr. Mac dedicated his time to not only teach us the language but also about the culture and customs of the Vietnamese people.

He worked within his community to educate them about policing in America and in Philadelphia in particular.

Mr. Mac saw opportunities to further increase and enhance his effectiveness in bringing the community and the police together by forming and serving on advisory councils and committees. To that end, he volunteered to serve as an advisor to Police Commissioner Charles Ramsey. While in that position, Mr. Mac asked me to help him establish the Philadelphia Police Asian-American Advisory Committee (PPAAAC). Not only did he ensure the Vietnamese community had representation, he also included all of the other Asian communities that wanted to participate (Korean, Philippine, Chinese, Indian, Pakistani, and others). These actions were a further testament to his genuine concern for all immigrants and his desire to help them in whatever way he could.

His many accomplishments include:

- Publishing *Rang Dong Sunrise,* a bilingual magazine (Vietnamese-English).
- Establishing a Vietnamese telephone directory in New York, New Jersey, and Pennsylvania.
- Establishing the Viet Nam Allied Veterans Association of Pennsylvania (VAVAP).
- Graduating from Temple University with a degree in electrical engineering.
- Establishing the Vietnamese United National Association of Greater Philadelphia (VUNA).

His record of service includes:

- Chairman of the Board of the Vietnamese American Community of the United States (VACUSA)

- Chairman of the Pan Asian Association of Greater Philadelphia
- Chairman of the Asian-American and Pacific Advisory Committee (AAPAC)
- Member of the Governor's Advisory Commission on Asian-American Affairs under Governor Tom Corbett
- Commissioner of the Mayor's Commission on Asian-American Affairs for Mayor Michael Nutter
- Member of the Philadelphia Police Commissioner's Advisory Council (PPAC)
- Chairman of the Philadelphia Police Asian-American Advisory Committee (PPAAAC)
- Member of the FBI Multicultural Advisory Committee
- Mr. John J. Gaittens
- Administrator, Law Enforcement Health Benefits, Inc.

INTRODUCTION II

Dr. Art Matson, PsyD

My journey to meet Mr. Quang Mac, formerly a ranking officer with a very important job in the Army of the Republic of South Viet Nam Military Command, began in an aging elementary school in Lawrence, Massachusetts, in 1998. At that time, as one of my requirements to complete my training for a doctorate in psychology, I was teaching common English idiomatic expressions to a group of South Vietnamese and Cambodian immigrants, both men and women. For the most part, they did not know each other. Every individual spoke the English language with a varying degree of competence. Many of the participants were also former officers in the Army of the Republic of South Viet Nam. The goal of the program was to ease their transition into everyday American life and culture.

Our meetings had been continuing for several months, and the group had developed trust with each other and with me. On one particular morning, a former major in the Vietnamese army, Mr. To Dang, near the end of the meeting, gently tugged at my right sleeve. I turned to him, and he tentatively asked, almost in a whisper, if the former officers (who had apparently previously talked together about the issue) might tell me of their experiences in the "camps." My response was great surprise, because I had no knowledge of the infamous reeducation camps established by the North Vietnamese after the fall of Saigon in 1975. I came to learn through the experiences of the men that these camps were in fact were very similar to the Nazi concentration camps of WWII. By mutual agreement, and with the sanction of my supervisor, the focus of the group shifted to the experiences of the former officers in the camps, as well as the experiences of their wives and children who were left behind.

One particular woman, Mrs. Nga Mac, informed me that her husband, a former officer, Mr. Van Mac, who was not participating in our group as he was employed, had also been imprisoned and wished to speak with me about his experiences. From our meetings, we became close friends, and he spoke to me about his brother, Mr. Quang Mac, who lived in Philadelphia, Pennsylvania. The latter individual had also been imprisoned in

1975 after the fall of Saigon, and Mr. Van Mac said he would put me in contact with his brother.

The following spring, I traveled to Philadelphia and met Mr. Quang Mac and his gracious wife in their very nice home. Graciousness and hospitality to visitors are prominent and engaging characteristics of the Vietnamese culture, and I felt very much at ease in their presence. Thus, our personal connection was established, and our friendship began. Subsequently, Mr. Mac greatly facilitated my research by introducing me to other former officers who spoke of their individual experiences in the camps with me.

Mr. Mac related to me one particular experience of barbaric torture by his North Vietnamese captors to extract sensitive information related to his job during the war, but the captive refused to cooperate. As punishment for his strength of character, courage, and unwillingness to provide secret information to the enemy, Mr. Mac was locked in a metal box used to ship equipment from the United States to Viet Nam. During the daytime, temperatures inside the metal box were excruciatingly hot, and many prisoners in similar situations as Mr. Mac died of heat exhaustion and dehydration. However, Mr. Mac survived through prayer and willpower, and in his own words related his torturous experience.

"You know that it is hot in Viet Nam, and they put me in the CONEX [Container Express] box about one month. I don't wear any clothes. It was very hot inside. We have water. I know the discipline of Kung Fu, and I know what is going on. If you live in a condition like that, you cannot drink so much water. You drink so much water, the sweat will come out and you will feel pain. I prayed and using the techniques of Kung Fu to sit on the floor and concentrating to pray and don't think about anything else for the day/nighttime, until I become tired and asleep."

Initially, all the prisoners were told that imprisonment was for a specified limit of three years, but as those years passed and no one was released, the reality of open-ended imprisonment became apparent. Mr. Mac had amply demonstrated his survival skills while imprisoned in the Conex box and continued to use them throughout his captivity. He survived while many other prisoners died from overwork and a poor diet. After more than five years of imprisonment, he was reunited with his family.

In January 1981, Mr. Mac and his family were resettled in Philadelphia, Pennsylvania, and began a new life, gradually integrating themselves into a different culture. He did so with the same energy and tenacity that exemplify his character. Mr. Mac used his considerable business and writing skills to begin publishing *Rang Dong Sunrise* magazine in 1982. The magazine was primarily for the Vietnamese community in Philadelphia, but it also had English commentary in order to grow the bond between two disparate cultures. Over the years, the magazine has thrived and become increasingly important in providing the Vietnamese community with important, topical information.

For many years, Mr. Mac has been and continues to be prominently involved in keeping alive the memory of South Viet Nam's struggle for freedom in ceremonies honoring both former Vietnamese and American military personnel, living and deceased. He is also politically active, not only in Philadelphia but throughout Pennsylvania, raising money for Vietnamese individuals seeking political office. Mr. Mac is a commissioner on the Governor's Advisory Commission on Asian-American Affairs and a member of the Mayor's Commission on Asian-American Affairs. He is also politically active in the Vietnamese American Voters League of Philadelphia and the Asian-American Political Action Committee.

Mr. Mac has been very active as a member of the Knights of Columbus, St. Helena Council #15687, and was eventually honored by becoming the elected head of the organization with the title of grand knight, in 2015. Using his leadership capabilities, Mr. Mac was responsible for the transportation needs of all Vietnamese clergy throughout the world who attended the Philadelphia conference. Mr. Mac carried out the monumental task in an exemplary manner, again demonstrating his strong organizational and leadership skills.

A reader of Mr. Mac's family history who is not of an Asian-American background may wonder why he has gone to such an extraordinary effort to compile and publish the history of his family. Throughout the history of the Vietnamese people, they have honored and venerated their ancestors, grounding the living into their family's past. Mr. Mac's primary goal is to honor and preserve the memory of his forbearers for the future generations of the Mac family and to inform other readers of his family's past.

Being asked by Mr. Mac to write this introduction is a great honor for me. I hold him in high regard for his steadfast dedication in many areas, for assisting and advancing the Asian-American community's welfare, and for bridging two cultures in shared respect.

Art Matson, PsyD

Preface

The Mac Dynasty began when the Le king transferred power to King Mac Đăng Dung, giving him the title of supreme king. Mạc Đăng Dung was born November 23, 1483, and he died August 22, 1541.

A. Mac Đăng Dung had nine children: Mạc Đăng Doanh, Mạc Phúc Hải, Mạc Phúc Nguyên, Mạc Mậu Hợp, Mạc Toàn, Mạc Kính Chỉ, Mạc Kính Cung, Mạc Kính Khoan, and Mạc Kính Vủ.

B. The Mac Dynasty held power in An Nam (what is now Viet Nam) for 150 years, losing the resulting battle after Lê Chiêu Thống requested that China attack the Mac Dynasty in northern An Nam. King Mạc Đăng Doanh's children moved to Binh Định (now Qui Nhơn Province) and finally to the delta region for resettlement. They remained there until escaping Viet Nam for Malaysia as boat people after April of 1975.

Because of the great distance between the northern and southern parts of the country, not all Mac descendants changed the family name. However, all the Mac families that lived in the north and central highlands of An Nam had to change their family name to Phạm, Hoàng, Trần, Nguyễn, etc. to prevent the Le king from killing them.

C. In 1954, the Geneva Accords divided Viet Nam into two countries: from the 17th parallel, the north belonged to the northern Communists, and the south belonged to the Republic of Viet Nam. On April 30, 1975, the northern Communists, supported by the Soviet Union and China, overthrew the Republic of Viet Nam (RVN) and all members of the military, civilians, and innocent people of the RVN had to go to the prisons that the Communists called reeducation camps. All families had to go to the jungle, which the Communists called the Economic Zone.

D. We fled our country to Malaysia in a small boat at the end of 1980 and resettled in Philadelphia with our children in 1981.

E. As great-great-grandchildren of the Mac Dynasty, we want to tell our children about the Mac Dynasty and teach them to keep our reputation and prestige.

F. As freedom fighters and advocates for democracy in Viet Nam, we want all the Vietnamese patriots who are living inside or outside Viet Nam to keep up their fight against the VN communists and the northern enemy until our country gains freedom and peace in Southeast Asia.

In conclusion, I would like to thank all my brothers who are helping me to complete my book. Especially, many thanks to Mr. Art Matson, Mr. Hoa Minh Truong, and Mr. John J. Gaittens, who have always supported my aspiration to tell the true history of Viet Nam's past.

Sincerely,
Quang Hong Mac
Raphael M.V. Mạc
April 30, 2020

Mr. & Mrs. Quang Hong Mac

Chapter 1

Results

April 30,1975

To continue to survive in the south of Viet Nam, the Mac family tried to adapt to the new society of the Mekong Delta from Đồng Nai to Mỹ Tho (Định Tường), Vĩnh Long (Cửu Long), Cần Thơ (Phong Dinh), and Cà Mau (An Xuyên). However, due to mismanagement, the Vietnamese communists (VC) had infiltrated the high-ranking government offices. Therefore most of the planned operations failed, such as Lam Son 719 in Laos. The VC knew our plans before we even started. Even the US government withdrew their troops, but the Vietnamese army continued fighting the North Viet Nam Communists until General Dương Văn Minh surrendered.

The purpose of this book is to gather the experiences of Vietnamese survivors of the reeducation camps, and from those stories ascertain their coping strategies, the influences of Vietnamese culture in those strategies, and the meaning the ex-prisoners attributed to those experiences. This portion of this story examines coping, culture, and meaning using the qualitative methodology previously outlined. The writer followed the Vietnamese practice of identifying individuals by their role names, which at the same time provides the anonymity several participants requested. Pertinent demographics are provided.

1

There were broad similarities in the former prisoners' descriptions of where they went or were transported by their captors, beginning with their return home after the fall of Saigon in April 1975 and continuing until their eventual release. Once the men left the relative safety of their homes, they were required to adapt to increasingly hostile circumstances. Each circumstance was distinctly different and more challenging than the preceding one, which required each man to become proficient in coping in a variety of ways in order to survive. The men learned to cope singularly and cooperatively. They used their intellects and their bodies. They coped overtly and covertly. The Vietnamese culture influenced their coping, and throughout their ordeal, the men laughed, cried, despaired, and hoped.

A portion of the results of this story, the descriptions of how each man coped and his emotional experiences, was grouped around each of the shared circumstances. These circumstances, which united the men in a shared journey, were the return home after the war's end, the reeducation collection point, the journey to the north, the reeducation camps, and finally the release. None of these men survived by chance, although some attributed it to that.

What is apparent throughout the narratives is that the men overcame the lethargy of earlier physical and emotional insults brought on by the shock of defeat and imprisonment, and began, somewhat hesitatingly at first, to learn to cope. By trial and error, and by observing other's successes and failures, these men devised methods of coping that allowed them to survive in an environment where so many of their comrades perished.

Finally, the meaning these men created to try to understand their predicament to sustain themselves throughout their ordeal and fit the experience into their current lives was discussed.

The Wanderers

All the participants were incarcerated in reeducation camps. All but one were former military officers who served at various times in the Army of the Republic of South Vietnamese (ARVN). The lone civilian is a Catholic priest who was arrested and incarcerated on the charge of sedition.

Their current ages range between fifty-two and seventy-five. The shortest period of incarceration was one year, and the longest was seventeen years. Most of the men are married with numerous children, some born in the former South Viet Nam and others in the United States. Many have relatives remaining in Viet Nam. Eleven individuals are Buddhist. Seven of are Catholic, and one is a Baptist. The roles the men adopted before incarceration included that of a military physician, pilot, priest, a retired officer turned politician, and a medical retiree (diabetes). Others serving on active duty at the time of the demobilization were an administrative officer, a psychological warfare officer, a maintenance officer, a police officer, and several officers of the line (e.g., company and battalion commanders). Most lived within the general camp population for the duration of their sentences. However, one former high-ranking combat officer spent five years in an isolation cell, and the Catholic priest was isolated for almost two years. Two men attempted escape, and one succeeded. Several of the men were wounded in combat, some multiple times. Others were injured during their incarceration. Some reported enduring emotional scars. All starved, and at one time or another during their time in the camps faced imminent death and survived.

The Return Home

For several days in the early spring of 1975, the ARVN had been retreating out of the highlands down coastal roads choked with civilians toward the supposed security of the Saigon defenses. Chaos was everywhere. Inexorably, the last vestiges of discipline dissolved, and once-cohesive units of battle-hardened men dispersed, each man taking his own escape route. The former soldiers became civilians again—sons, husbands, and fathers seeking to protect and be protected by their families. Now-useless uniforms were discarded in the vain hope that the former wearer could melt into the refugee mass and not be discovered by the new authorities.

That hope was forlorn, because their names and addresses had already been compiled by local Viet Cong cadres, to be used when the South Vietnamese government fell.

The collapse of the South Vietnamese government on April 30, 1975, was made official by the acting president, General Dương Văn Minh, known as "Big Minh," but his radio announcement was a mere formality.

Even in the chaotic retreat, most of the officers continued to believe they could eventually prevail if the United States intervened. When that did not occur, the former soldiers gradually gave up hope. The official radio announcement of capitulation left many of the men stunned and sad.

For one of the survivors, a former air force administrator, the news evoked painful, emotional memories. "Yes, the radio. I was sad. I was very, very sad."

Instinctively, the men retreated into their only remaining security, their families. Many of the higher commanders escaped the country, some with their families, and their example was not lost on the junior officer corps. Many of those men also contemplated escape, but the cultural press of family obligations and the lack of wherewithal to leave Viet Nam as a family dissuaded them. To leave the family behind was almost unthinkable.

A survivor who had been a helicopter pilot remarked, "I decided because of my children. I couldn't go and leave my wife with the responsibility to take care and raise the children in a very bad situation."

An air force maintenance officer understood this obligation as one strengthened by his culture when he spoke of his "filial duty in the Eastern culture" to protect his family. A certain degree of poignancy, a romanticism inured in the Vietnamese culture, also weighed against escape without the family.

A former battalion commander articulated such sentiments. "Most of Vietnamese people, we are sentimental, so that I wanted to come back home to see my wife and my children and see what happened to them before I made my decision."

In those dark days, there were still darker moments in which culture may have played a role. There were suicides of former commanders who were overcome by the same sense of defeat.

The battalion commander, experiencing that same shame, contemplated his own death as atonement. "If we follow the Vietnamese culture, we must die right away after April 15, 1975, because we were so young, we were taught that we never surrender ... You know, the first day when I come home, I prepare myself for suicide. I prepare everything, but my wife told me, 'You are Catholic. You cannot commit suicide.'"

Throughout the country, former officers and their families nervously awaited the orders of their Communist victors. A retired soldier turned politician spoke of his fears, an emotion which was experienced by several of his brother officers. "That is what the Oriental people, especially the Vietnamese people, believe. They never, never go to jail. They are very scared of jail, even before 1975. We have one sentence: '*One day in prison, that is almost the same as if lived outside one hundred years.*'"

The Reeducation Collection Point

When the summons came via radio, its message was couched in terms calculated to reassure the officers and their families that it would be just two to three weeks of introduction to the requirements of the new regime. They were told to bring clothes and food sufficient for that time period. Many of the former officers, breathing a collective sigh of relief, went willingly. Their understanding of what reeducation entailed varied, running the gamut from that of benign, personal improvement to permanent thought alteration.

One survivor, a physician, believed it had to do with personal improvement. "They want us to become good men. That's why they call it a reeducation camp."

A former A-37 pilot attributed the more sinister purpose for reeducation. "I think that they try to clear your brain, to wash your brain, because they know you are different."

For some of the men, reeducation remained misunderstood. Even a year after he had been incarcerated, the politician still was not sure what reeducation meant. "The first year, I don't know about it. I really don't know."

Some former officers arrived before their required report time with the thought to begin reeducation early and end early. A minority was less hopeful. The older officers who had fought first against the French, then the Viet Minh, and finally the North Vietnamese and Viet Cong, knowing the mindset of their enemies, attempted to steel themselves and their families for a more somber reality.

The air force administrator told his wife on departing for reeducation that she would not see him again. "You remember. This day is a last day of my days. I know how the Communists treat me under the new regime, so I think I will be dead in the prison."

The air force A-37 pilot remarked, "I just put on the worst scenario. Maybe some violence, people like the guards doing something. You try to protect them. They kill you."

The former officers and government officials reported to different locations throughout the country, such as old military bases or high schools, based on their rank or government position. New arrivals were comforted by the large numbers of their former colleagues who were also present and by the disarming messages of their captors that they all would be released in a short time.

At the same time, the fall from positions of authority became all too apparent to the newly made prisoners. They were crowded together in rooms designed for half of their number. Young peasant boys dressed in baggy black uniforms carrying AK-47s guarded them. The prisoners could not eat, bathe, or go to the bathroom without permission.

The A-37 pilot described his personal distress resulting from his loss of position. "Because when you go down into the bottom of your life . . . even the young soldier, he punish you. He order you to do something, and you feel nothing."

As the time limit set by the communists passed and the men were not released, the reality of their situation became increasingly evident, that they were indeed prisoners. The brief emotional interlude of hope flickered and then faded, replaced by disbelief that this situation could really be as bad as it appeared to be. This reversal of fortune was sometimes overwhelming, and the helplessness of their situation emotionally paralyzed many of the men.

A former air force F-5 pilot articulated what many of the prisoners must have felt. "The unreality of it all, I was in a limbo situation. I was not really awake or asleep. Yes, it was inconceivable, like a dream."

Others, like the air force maintenance officer, became depressed. "When I was in prison, I hoped my children could have an education, because now my life was destroyed."

For the men, the first casualty had been the loss of hope. Human casualties followed as desperate men attempted escape and were shot, or escaped, were later captured, and then shot. Those executions were graphic examples to the prisoners of the punishment for attempting escape.

A former company commander reported on the executions he witnessed. "They killed them in front of us!"

Food shortages occurred as the prisoners' supplies shrank and the prison cadres did not make up the shortfall. Being continually hungry became a new and uncomfortable experience for the men. A few resourceful prisoners attempted to take charge of their dwindling food stocks and initiate a ration system.

A young physician was one of the men who helped organize the rationing. "When I was three months in the first place, we got a one-month supply, and we extended that to three months."

Later, in the northern camps, finding enough to eat to keep from starving to death would become the consuming activity of most of the prisoners.

The ordeal of personal history writing began. The Communists required each prisoner to write a life history with particular emphasis on his military role in the war. These histories were used by the North Vietnamese cadres to determine the degree of culpability of each prisoner and consequently his length of stay in reeducation. The Communists required that these histories be written over and over again until they were acceptable. The seemingly most benign military of civilian occupation had to be presented so as to demonstrate the prisoner's responsibility in the deaths of Viet Cong and North Vietnamese soldiers. Thus, the air force administrator who dealt with personnel issues confessed to being responsible for their deaths. This torturing exercise presented the prisoners with two possibilities: tell the truth and hope that being honest would be seen by his captors as a sign of good faith and a willingness to accept reeducation, or lie by minimizing involvement with the war effort.

To induce the prisoners to tell the Communists, they let them know that they had captured the IBM tapes containing each man's service record. However, the Communists did not inform the prisoners that they were unable to decode the tapes. Most prisoners thought the best strategy was to tell the truth regarding their roles and even take bogus secured methods, or those with much to hide lied. However, lying had to remain uniform over time. A prisoner caught in a lie might add time to his reeducation and would certainly result in a beating or an isolation cell.

The soldier turned politician chose the second way. "I tried to remember every detail, every sentence. I try to write short sentences from memory. You give them, and then tomorrow they ask you again. If you change it, you have a problem."

The air force A-37 pilot also wrote a fictitious history. "If you feel they don't know anything, then just tell lies. Just do whatever you want, but keep in mind to keep the reports uniform. Next time you say the same thing."

Chapter 2

The Journey to the North

Most often it came in the dead of night: the shrill blast of whistles, the beating of gongs, and the yelling of guards. The sleepy and dazed men were ordered to pack their belongings. Hurriedly, they threw together their few possessions, making sure to safeguard any food or medicine they may have hidden from the guards, and stumbled into the road where Molotowa, Russian trucks belching diesel fumes, awaited them. Jammed into the trucks with the canvas tightly secured to prevent looking out, the prisoners were driven on circuitous routes to their destination. No one talked because of the menacing presence of young guards with submachine guns, but they all mentally questioned where they were headed. Finally, the convoy halted, and the tarps were thrown back. The prisoners found themselves dockside. In front of them were commercial freighters chartered by the Communists, and the message became clear to all: they were going to the north.

The maintenance officer remembered how he felt at this turn of events. "Well, sad, because we had to leave the south."

The A-37 pilot was more sanguine. "Actually, I felt like we would go to the north sometime. I just prepared myself for the worst case."

The prisoners stumbled up the gangway, brought aboard ship, and then forced below decks. Hatch covers were toggled down above the men, and sudden darkness enveloped them.

For the maintenance officer, the memory of that hellish passage remained vivid. "They put you in the hold of the boat, and they cover it. They don't tell us, but we know. Among us, we have a pilot, an air force pilot. We also had navy officers."

With their expertise, the men were able to tell the ship's course by using the movement of slivers of sunlight through holes in the hatch cover. The sea journey in the hold of the ship was excruciating for the men packed together in darkness and overpowering heat, breathing fetid air permeated by diesel fumes.

The air force pilot continued his story: "*Song Huong*, a commercial ship, carried us for four days and three nights. At least ten prisoners were dead in the ship hold by suffocation." He picked up the narrative as they made port in the north. "Almost six hundred prisoners were disembarked at Hai Phong Harbor. At the time of debarking from boats, we had been disgracefully welcomed by North Vietnamese uniformed secret police."

From the docks, the prisoners, surrounded by police escorts and attack dogs, were marched through the streets of Hai Phong to the railhead for the continuation of their relocation. The air force administrator related the degradation he and the other prisoners experienced at the hands of their North Vietnamese captors. He reported how the prisoners were jammed into filthy cattle cars that were open to the weather, then taken by barges across rivers, and finally marched to their destination, which was located in mountainous terrain close to the Chinese border.

11

The Reeducation Camp

The bedraggled column of prisoners had been marched for some miles around rice paddies recently harvested, or if the guards were more sadistic, through them (the sharp remains of the rice stalks would cut the men's legs). Leaving the fields behind, the men climbed into the forested mountains, where the temperature became noticeably cooler. Finally, the fatigued men were brought to a halt. According to two sources, the prisoners were very surprised and confused when they halted, because there were no buildings—nothing!

The battalion commander, one of the sources, commented on the situation. "When we arrived, there was no camp. We cannot call it a camp, because when we first came into the jungle, there was no camp, so we must build it. We make a prison for a prisoner!"

The air force administrator provided a second account of halting and finding no facilities to house the men. He related sleeping in a recently harvested rice paddy the first night at the site. In the morning, he and his fellow prisoners were marched into the forest to cut trees and bamboo to build huts. That was the first time many of the men had felled trees or worked in construction. The work was unusually hard because the cutting tools were only machetes, and the mountainous terrain made it dangerous.

While there had been individual attempts at coping with their situation before arriving at the camps, the men had been purposely kept off-balance by the North Vietnamese to prevent rebellion or escape. Now they were presented with a situation far different from their previous lives and forced to learn how to survive or die. Because of their middle-class backgrounds, very few of the men had the basic skills needed to cut trees to build barracks or to cultivate fields, but they had to learn construction and farming techniques in a hurry.

The air force maintenance officer described his initial feelings, first of anxiety and then a calmness, when he regarded the enormity of the tasks ahead of him and the other prisoners. In time, the surviving prisoners became proficient in completing assignments.

The air force administrator chronicled their increasing work skills. "Today you must dig six holes. But how can you get started? It's not easy. The first day we try to dig with the rake, the six holes. One month later, twenty holes. After one year, two years, every day one hundred holes. You believe it! But every month after that, we get better and better."

Besides the terrain, the weather also presented challenges because it was much colder in winter, and the men were acclimated to the warmer weather of the south. To compound the problem, they did not have adequate clothing. By that time, the clothing they had left was tattered, and the physician related that the men were forced to fashion garments from burlap sandbags.

Even in their precarious situation, there were acts of kindness. The regimental commander described how he assisted a freezing comrade. "I had a sweater, and I saw a young prisoner, and I tell him, 'Why do you have no shirt on your body?' He says, 'I have no clothes,' so I took off my sweater and gave it to him."

As before, the North Vietnamese controlled and tantalized the hungry and cold prisoners with hopes of freedom, intimating that if they worked hard they would be released sooner. Along with other desperate prisoners, the army battalion commander wanted to believe his captors. "The first three years we were surviving, hoping that we would be released sooner."

The company commander shared that hope, based on the Communists telling the prisoners that they would be released in three years. There were no releases.

In the beginning, nighttime was often the worst. The prisoners stumbled and shuffled through a day attaining their work quota, too busy to think. At night, the cold and hungry prisoners lay close together for warmth on reed mats, seeking solace in thoughts of home and family. Many of the officers reported that thinking of family could also bring thoughts of deep concern for their welfare. Such thoughts were distracting at best, and at worst could lead to depression. Yet, being human, they still remembered family.

The helicopter pilot related that if he were not distracted by the work, his thoughts drifted home and he became emotional. "Because when I have free time, I remember all my family, my children, my wife, and I probably cry."

The F-5 pilot reported his policy of not thinking about his family to avoid unhappy feelings. "If you think about your family, you have no peace of mind."

The Prisoner's Outer World

As time passed, the camp was completed. Some prisoners remained, while others marched away to build additional camps. The battalion commander was posted to a construction crew and spent much of his time in captivity moving about North Viet Nam building camps.

The prisoner's physical world was geographically circumscribed, made up of his worksite, his camp, and his barracks. The typical camp was sited in the valley between mountains and near running water. The camp most often was rectangular, surrounded by a wooden stockade and razor wire and manned by guards in corner watchtowers. There was only one entrance, and the camp commander's hut was located beside the gate.

The camp barracks were roughly built structures, each home to thirty to forty prisoners. There might be ten to twelve barracks in each camp. In the middle of a barracks was a jail in which one could urinate, and hanging from the ceiling was a kerosene lantern. The latrine was positioned outside in the space between barracks. The men slept in rows on matting on top of planking. There was barely enough room for a prisoner to roll over. However, in the winter, having other prisoners close by provided a measure of warmth. At night, the barracks were locked, and anyone who needed to use the outside latrine must first get the attention of a roving guard.

Generally, the prisoners' camp was part of a larger complex of camps that radiated from a central location like spokes of a wheel. The camp complex provided for certain economies, like relatively easy administration and supply. The guards, usually drafted from the local population, were frequently moved from one camp to the next so there would be no possibility of fraternization with "enemies of the state." Most of the men reported no personal contact with their guards. To thwart the establishment of group resistance cells and individual escapes, each prisoner was frequently moved between camps. Thus, there was a continuous shuffle of guards and prisoners throughout the camp complex.

Work

The workday began early with the preparation of food to be carried to the worksite, followed by an assembly in the barracks yard for a prisoner count. The prisoners were then marched to

15

the worksite. Sometimes the site might be as much as a two-hour walk from the camp. The work continued until dusk, when the prisoners were marched back to the camp.

Again, there was a roll call. In the evening after a meager meal, the prisoners attended political classes and sat in small groups and criticized each other's performance. Several of the officers reported that criticizing comrades was the hardest camp rule for them to follow because Vietnamese culture discourages public criticism. The men worked six days a week and sometimes also on Sunday. Sunday work was supposed to be voluntary for those individuals who wanted to work for the "Socialist State," but in practice, if work was scheduled, everyone worked. At other times, prisoners used Sunday to wash clothes and search for food.

Antennas

As time passed, the prisoners began to regularize their lives within the primitive conditions in which they existed. When there was free time in the evening in the barracks, after classes or on Sundays, the prisoners swapped gossip, conspired, and lifted each other's spirit in small, tightly knit groups. Additionally, they sang songs, wrote poetry, surreptitiously studied religious tracts, learned languages, read letters from home, and wrote letters (when that became possible).

The furtiveness was necessary due to the ubiquitous "antennas," turncoat prisoners who reported on their comrades for extra rations. A former army ranger described the secrecy required. "Don't talk. Don't criticize. If you have a dear friend, you can talk, but alone, because the environment makes you not trust anybody!"

Several of the men reported how they dealt with the antennas. The battalion commander reported that he heard rumors that antennas had been killed.

The army ranger was part of a collective coping strategy that dealt with the problem. "We cannot beat them up, no, but we don't talk with them. We separated them from us, let them feel lonely." That was important because in the Vietnamese culture men form strong social bonds with each other. For a man, being isolated from his society, even one composed of prisoners, was a steep price to pay for extra rations.

Medicine

The prisoners were very much aware that they had to attempt to keep the camp and barracks sanitary to prevent contagions, even though in actuality there was little they could do except clean the latrines. The raw waste from this source was collected and mixed into the garden soil. All the former prisoners reported becoming sick at one time or another. Several of the former prisoners reported receiving aid from former physicians of the ARVN, but that was unusual. Generally, for the sick there was poor medical assistance available at best. Mostly, the prisoners relied on each other and their husbanded stock of aspirin or quinine. In fact, quinine became the drug most often self-prescribed for almost every ailment.

The F-5 pilot described its common usage. "Most of the time, our relatives would send tablets of quinine for prevention of malaria, and we would save them for a remedy against any sickness."

Each camp had a dispensary, but it was more a place to rest rather than to heal. There was very little medicine in the dispensary, and what was available was of dubious quality, as it came from the Soviet Union. Even the prison guards, when ill, would ask the prisoners if they had medications from the south rather than risk taking medicines supplied by the Soviet Union.

Chapter 3

Communication

Of vital interest to every prisoner was what was going on in the world that might influence his situation. When letter writing became possible, the prisoners wanted to be able to write what was on their minds, but the censors would not allow it. In fact, if the prisoner reported any negative information, he would be punished.

The former policeman described the dilemma of the letter writer: "The most difficult thing to comply with was that I want to wire a letter to my wife. I can't tell the truth. I can't say I am hungry. I have to write what I am not thinking at this time. I must write what the policy tells me to write. That is hard, hard!"

However, resourceful prisoners and their wives devised codes in order to trade information. The air force maintenance officer described the code he and his wife concocted: "That's a huge problem. But our wives in the south, they were very, very clever, very smart. They write a letter to us saying, 'At home, Uncle My (American) will marry Miss Hoa (China) very soon.' We analyze it. Well, there is an agreement between the Americans and Chinese."

The importance of receiving letters from home to keep up one's morale was emphasized by the regimental commander who corresponded with his wife. "She kept sending me letters. Once in a while I got her mail. It was good for my morale. She always say, 'Cau, you have to remain healthy so that someday we can reunite. Don't do anything stupid.' I trusted her, and she helped a lot."

Several of the men reported there were other ways to learn about the outside world. Secret radios were acquired by hook or crook, secreted, and the Voice of America (VOA) or the British Broadcasting Company (BBC) was monitored. Because of the antennas, there was the ever-present danger of exposure.

The air force pilot related one such close call: "There was the miracle of the radio. A radio was hidden in a can with just a cloth over it. The guards came in to search for it. We had to distract the guards so they wouldn't find it. I was third to be questioned, and they said, 'What are you doing?' I said, 'Adjusting my sandals,' and while the guards were looking away, my friend took the radio out of the can and put it high on the shelf."

In a second account, the company commander related how the guards were tricked out of their radio. According to him, a guard heard that one of the prisoners had previously served in the ARVN Signal Corps and requested that the prisoner fix a broken radio. The resourceful prisoner informed the guard that the radio would take several weeks to fix. In that time, the prisoners were able to listen to the outside world. Each time the guard came to check on the repair, the prisoner would disable the radio. The prisoners were able to maintain the charade for three months.

Free Time

Some prisoners used their free time to learn languages, most often English. Many of the men had either learned English as a child in school or later when they were serving in the ARVN and attended English language schools run by the United States military. Again, one had to be careful, because if reported, severe punishment was in store for the prisoner.

The A-37 pilot told of his English self-study. "I learn English. You don't tell anybody you are learning English. Just like somebody that make a poem, they have to hide it. They write it down, they remember it, and they destroy it. Chance to use English later."

The helicopter pilot related that he learned English during his spare time reading old maintenance manuals left by the United States Army. For him, it was also a way to distract himself from worrying about his family.

There were only a few reports of prisoners exercising. The physician, who was proficient in woodworking, was one such person. "I tried to exercise with a primitive thing I made." Another report came from the priest, whose only form of exercise was walking in his isolation cell. The final report came from the air force pilot, who lifted homemade weights in the barracks at night.

Activities that promoted coping and were approved by the camp authorities were group singing and the playing of musical instruments. Flutes could be fashioned from pieces of tiny bamboo. The physician built guitars and taught other prisoners how to play. Individual and group singing was very popular, but the singer(s) had to be careful about the lyrics they sang.

The regimental commander explained why that was necessary. "I sang the 'green' songs. Communists classify songs in three different categories: The red songs are Communists. The yellow songs are for the South Vietnamese. The green songs are in between, not for the Communists and not for the south. The green songs are about the country, love stories, etc."

Also, the prisoners were avid players of dominos, cards, and checkers.

Mistakes

At times the prisoners coped well with their situations, and at other times they were less able to do so. Losing patience could cause the men to make serious errors, which would put them at risk for punishment. At times using humor to lighten a burden could cause trouble for a prisoner if he was overheard by the antennas. Just speaking one's mind would likely result in punishment if the prisoner was reported.

The army ranger commented that his particular difficulty was being too talkative. The regimental commander provided another example that highlighted the need to keep silent. "I was chained once because I tell something against Communism, and the antennas reported to the guard."

On the other hand, the regimental commander noted that being too quiet could also spell trouble. He reported a typical belief held by the Communist cadres concerning the quiet prisoner. "He is quiet outside, so something must be in his mind."

Controlling thoughts and emotions became a safety requirement for the prisoners because uncontrolled thoughts might translate into dangerous facial expressions like anger, which betrayed the prisoner.

The helicopter pilot reported an experience with not controlling his anger and the very serious repercussions that might have followed. One day while working in the vegetable garden, he became angry because the best tomatoes were taken by the guards. In anger, he picked one off the vine and smashed it with his foot. The helicopter pilot was taken before the Communist cadre and threatened with death. Thinking quickly, he reported that he had destroyed the tomato to encourage the others to grow faster. That saved him. He remarked that, "After that time, I know if I don't control my anger, I will be in trouble."

Uncontrolled thoughts of family could bring on deep sorrow or make the prisoner physically sick, as the army ranger explained. "I don't know what is happening to my family. Do my children go to school every day? Do they have enough to eat? Thoughts like that could make you sick too."

Food

Hunger was an ever-present sensation for the prisoners, and for most of the prisoners the search for food to augment their meager rations was a continuing quest. The exception was those men who worked in the kitchen. Those jobs were usually given to prisoners who had Communist relatives. In the camps, the prisoner's diet was radically changed. The prisoner's stomach, used to traditional Vietnamese food, was abruptly assaulted by the course feed of grains, which now became a staple of their diet along with garden-grown manioc. There was very little rice and almost no meat, except on Communist holidays and during the Tet celebration. As one would expect, such a diet produced diarrhea, and if the prisoner became weaker through dehydration, dysentery was a likely complication. Dysentery could also be contracted when starving men ate raw vegetables fertilized with their own excrement.

Dysentery could kill in more than one way. The physician explained how that transpired. "During the evening hours, you have to sit and write, and only one person can go to move the bowels over there. So he's so urgent, and he was shot."

The air force administrator described how they did so. "Guards received the first level. Later, some ask for food from the prisoners when food comes from family. 'A,' the best workers and camp personnel, get eighteen kilos per month. 'B,' average workers, twelve kilos per month, and 'C,' lazy workers, nine kilos per month. In isolation, three kilos per month."

There was a strong temptation in the beginning for the prisoners to attempt to achieve the *A* level for the increased rations, but increased labor for the increased food could be a risky trade. The policeman described what happened to some of the men who worked very hard: "The young, they work hard and get twenty-one kilos of rice. They work too hard. When they get sick, they get thirteen kilos. That weakens them and makes them more ill."

He also observed, "We recognized that the young die more than the old. If we eat fifteen kilos, we don't survive!"

There was a cultural inclination for the prisoners to work hard, in addition to it being required of them by the camp administration. Several of the prisoners reported that they had learned from their parents' example.

The regimental commander was their spokesperson. "I think they were hard-working people, so they set a good example for me."

The F-5 pilot, while agreeing with the regimental commander, provided an additional explanation. "We were so poor, so it was easy. The amplitude of the fall from where we were to here."

The prisoners developed a series of coping skills to deal with their starvation and to conserve their dwindling strength. Often reported by the prisoners was the conservation of the breakfast ration, which was then eaten with lunch. The result was a sensation of fullness, which temporarily assuaged the prisoner's hunger. Prisoners working in the garden were able to find earthworms and grasshoppers to eat. However, they had to do so surreptitiously because they were guarded. Another drawback in garden work was that the prisoners were unable to rest except at designated meal breaks. The better jobs were in the mountains, and the stronger prisoners attempted to join those work details. There were risks as well as benefits in such a strategy. The jobs were dangerous—cutting and dragging timber down the mountainsides.

The battalion commander, through an interpreter, told how dangerous it was on the mountain. "When someone fell off, they became handicapped. Another time they were asked to go up the mountain and they dropped a log and killed two people."

However, the prisoners were generally unaccompanied by guards, so they could spend time searching for small game, wild manioc, and mushrooms, being careful to avoid the poisonous varieties. If they were cautious, the prisoners could also build cooking fires.

The regimental commander commented on the strategy. "If you are strong, you like this job because you can search for something extra for food. You can get a snake or a frog."

The A-37 pilot told of his experience foraging in the mountains. "So they pick up when they go, and they see some insects, little ones, and snatch and chop and protect everything. They put them on the fire and cook them."

Another strategy was to more than fulfill the day's work requirement so that on the succeeding day the prisoners could rest and devote their time to searching for food.

Many of the camps had been located in thinly populated areas of North Viet Nam. The indigenous people, the Tay, the Giao Man, and the Nam Dinh, who were earlier persecuted by the North Vietnamese, were friendly and provided food in secret places to the prisoners.

The air force administrator described how they aided him. "They respected me. They gave me a lot of food."

Food smuggled into the barracks always had to be kept hidden from the guards. The air force administrator explained why. "Every month or two months there was an inspection. We must bring all of our property. They check everything."

The food must also be concealed from other prisoners, except for close friends. The physician explained how hunger could turn men against each other, make them act less than human. "Even people fighting for a piece of rotten meat. We not ourselves anymore. The main thing is that our stomach is full. That is the best thing to do. We don't care about anything else."

Even the strongest and the most resourceful foragers could not avoid the inexorable loss of body fat and muscle, as their caloric intake never equaled what they expended in exertion. Without mirrors, they could not see the extent of the ravages of starvation on their own bodies, but the prisoners could see slow death working in their friends. Understanding that their way of working, overproducing the quota, would eventually cause death, several men reported adopting a different work strategy.

The battalion commander related what changed. "We don't work so hard like we did before, because we know exactly that if we work harder, we will kill ourselves. We still do what they want but at the lower rate."

The A-37 pilot formulated his own plan. "I think the purpose here, I try to keep myself safe so one day I will be released."

The majority of the prisoners believed that self-discipline in all areas of their camp lives, especially concerning what they ate, was central to their survival. Additionally, to eat uncooked food grown in ground fertilized by raw human waste was courting death.

The company commander spoke for many prisoners. "I myself found a little something to help me to survive. I can cope with the situation. I chose what to cook."

Forgetting Hunger

While working in the mountains was advantageous for foraging, there were more subtle benefits from being away from the guards. The gnawing hunger could be forgotten for a time when the prisoners could socialize with each other. Keeping in mind the possible presence of antennas, the prisoners were able to talk to close friends about what they were thinking and feeling. In addition, they found things that were funny in their existence.

The physician sought out the forest work to share his feelings with friends. "We know who our close friends are. We can share that feeling when we work together in the jungle."

Laughter could also dampen hunger pangs. The F-5 pilot commented on humor's emotional, therapeutic effects. "It's kind of a relief from tension, so they joke about things."

The air force maintenance officer reported that he accidentally caught a picture of Ho Chi on fire in the outhouse while trying to keep warm. Because the prisoner was surrounded by so much death, it was not surprising that he could find humor in the morbid.

The former officer turned politician related a funny story:

One of the teachers, a former officer who was assigned as a teacher to a high school, one tall guy and one short guy. They assigned two of them to go to the jungle, but at that time, the two catch the Communists with their guard down. The tall guy told the small guy, "Okay, I cut this, the tall one, and you cut the small one."

They didn't know that the two guards overheard them. They thought the two guys were trying to kill them. There was a misunderstanding. They thought these guys were going to kill them, and they shot them both!

Experiencing strong emotions like hate was another way to temporarily forget about being hungry. While the majority of the prisoners reported they did not use hatred of the Communists to survive, some did.

The company commander turned his hatred of communism into humorous relief. "Because I hate communism, I think of something to laugh at them, like to make a joke on their policy."

For some of those officers, like the A-37 pilot, who used their hatred to survive, their sentiments did not pertain to their guards. "Because I know the low people. They just obey the high-ranking people."

Using hate to cope could exact a price. The F-5 pilot spoke of the lurking danger in using hate to survive. "I think the first or second year, I said that if I ever get out of the camp, when I see any Communists, the only thing they deserve is to be killed. But I realize if you had hate in yourself, it is like poison. It just grows. So I think why not go higher than that. Those guys are not responsible. They are only the tools, the pawns."

Several prisoners, like the A-37 pilot, spoke of the guards being just like them. "Just like we joke, the prisoner out and the prisoner in. Guards are prisoners too."

Chapter 4

Role Playing

The men played the role of prisoner. Taking up that role was made easier due to their parents' teachings and the Vietnamese culture with its ingrained Confucian ethos of the importance of playing the prescribed role. One in which they did so was in setting out the camp rules, appeals to do good labor and maintain good discipline.

The helicopter pilot understood his role was to "be a good prisoner." For him, that meant being very cooperative, nonviolent, and obeying orders. The policeman related what his parents had taught him. "In any situation, be patient. Accept what occurs. Believe in doing good."

The guards also had a role to play. The physician described that role. "They have the duty, the responsibility to keep us under control."

The intelligence officer explained what happened when the prisoner did not fulfill his role. "When they beat someone, that one must have some serious fault."

For other officers, like the F-5 pilot, their role as prisoners was linked with their destiny. "I tell you the truth, I don't know, but there is something beyond. People say God, destiny. It's beyond what you have control of."

The policeman accepted his role. "We accepted our fate."

Family Visits

Beginning in 1982, the Communist authorities realized that not only were the camps not self-sufficient, but that they were declining in sufficiency due to prisoner deaths. To stabilize the situation, they began allowing family members to visit the prisoners and encouraged them to bring foodstuffs and medicine. Such a trip to North Viet Nam was very difficult and required at least a three-day transit. The family visits were very infrequent and painfully short, usually VOA one hour, divided into two half-hour sessions, with the Communist guards present. No matter its length, the visit provided a needed boost to the prisoner's morale.

The former air force administrator described how spirits could be raised. "When we heard the information from the family, we know someday, not too long, we will be released."

Since the guards and camp cadre were fed from the same prison gardens and later shared with his close friends, sometimes the visits came at a terrible price. The former soldier turned politician tells about the high personal cost of one such family visit. "One case I never forget, the lady came for a visit with her husband. He (camp deputy commander, namely T.B.) saw the lady and told her, 'If you want to see your husband, you have to sleep with me.' When she saw her husband and told him about it, he can do nothing!"

From the central part of Viet Nam to the prison was a thousand kilometers. Not only food and medicine, but news of the outside world arrived when families came to visit. The former A-37 pilot described some sources of the news brought by visitors. "The good news was when someone not in my family came to visit some of my friends, and they listened outside of the camp to the VOA and BBC."

QUANG HONG MAC (RAPHAEL M.V. MAC)

Resistance

Despite the frequent searches, abrupt moves between camps, and the presence of the ubiquitous antennas, some prisoners actively resisted their captors, as well as planned and executed escapes. Individual and organized resistance was fostered by a strong sense of patriotism among many of the men.

One such man was the army ranger. "Someday we would reorganize, and we have to survive now. We waited for that day!"

The priest came right to the point. "Before I was a Catholic, I was a Vietnamese!"

For some prisoners, like the A-37 pilot, patriotism became idealized. "If you still have the doctrines that you had, you have to believe in the republic and liberty; one day you will get them."

For other officers, like the air force administrator, patriotism leavened by culture was joined to a nostalgic ideal, a South Vietnamese Camelot. "Because I think it is my duty. We have to protect our land of our ancestors, you know?"

Individual and group resistance took several forms as starving prisoners engaged in desperate acts. The company commander, seemingly at the end of his endurance, exposed his chest and spoke out to the cadre, "Stop it! Stop it! I am too hungry to live, to live like this, and so it's better you kill me!"

The weakened air force maintenance officer related a story of a prisoner speaking out against the guards. "You see, if you the same age as my son, I would horsewhip you."

Individual prisoners, such as the company commander, planned for eventual escape. "I hide. When I work, I try to hide, to dig, to hide some food to try to escape, but it is not a success."

The former air force administrator, tired of writing phony statements to his wife that were acceptable to the censors,

30

challenged the cadre by writing, "I challenge you to never, never release me until the future!"

Prisoner resistance took on subtler forms. The military policeman resisted the basic premises of Communist reindoctrination. "I think they cannot reeducate us. I knew they could not reeducate us!"

The former maintenance officer attempted to indoctrinate his captors. "I saw that they were very young, so it was easy to talk to them."

Sometimes groups of prisoners resisted in song. The former company commander reported how they did it. "I knew a lieutenant colonel. He get the people together with him and sang some very famous songs, but they changed the words."

Groups of prisoners were equally furtive as they discussed resistance and escape. The soldier turned politician related one episode. "We had to select some of my best friends to talk about when we escape and what we are doing."

The air force administrator described another secret discussion. "They came to me and said, 'Colonel, we have to escape.' I said, No, don't go with me because somebody looks at me."

Incredibly, some starving prisoners organized a hunger strike. The policeman recounted what happened. "We try to strike. We put us in hunger. We did not eat. We ask them to return us to the south, but they don't. They put most of us in isolates. We keep asking them to return to the south. I knew a priest. He spent isolation in there, but when he was released from isolation, he cannot walk. He crawl."

Finally, prisoners were heartened and sustained by a belief in an organized military resistance to the Communists. The psychological warfare officer spoke about the resistance. "In prison, I heard about 'our fox.' That meant a lot of our soldiers were in the jungle fighting."

31

Chapter 5

Escape

Because of the dissolution of South Viet Nam, the prisoners lost the geographical entity to which they belonged, and that fact was not lost on the men. The air force pilot explained their predicament. "No homeland. Where do you escape to?"

The F-5 pilot expressed the same thought. "South Viet Nam no longer existed. That was the first lesson!"

Since there could be no assistance from their country, the prisoners realized there were no options except to depend on themselves. The A-37 pilot related that understanding. "So, we just depended on the group, the escape group."

The odds of successfully escaping from a northern camp were long. The prisoners found it difficult to store and hide emergency rations outside of the camp. For the starving prisoners, even to save a portion of a meager diet required an exceptionally strong will. Even with a food cache, once away from the camp, the escapees would be betrayed by their clothing and by the southern intonation of their language. Many times the Communist guards employed the local populace, who knew the surrounding country intimately, to hunt down the escapee. But starving men took the gamble, and just the hope of escape could keep some men alive.

The helicopter pilot was one such individual. "I don't have other strengths besides the idea of how to get out of prison. That help me a lot!"

He eventually escaped by commandeering a helicopter, picking up his family, and flying to safety in Thailand. He commented, "When I get the helicopter, I fly a few feet above the ground. Then they couldn't shoot at me. I tell you, that's the first time I fly that low altitude—and the last time!"

Another escapee, the air force pilot, was not successful. "I escaped twice from the first camp and returned in one day and didn't tell anyone. I escaped from a North Vietnamese camp, Hoang Lien Son, and was gone for thirteen days."

Punishment

Early in their captivity, the prisoners observed what happened to captured escapes: death by firing squad, by beating, or they were placed in isolation cells and starved to death.

The physician described an execution at his camp. "In the isolated area in Chi Lang, three of them Fo

Any time they captured the one who escaped, they jump on the chest of the escapee so that the escaped man will vomit blood. Sometimes they kill at night . . . all of the prisoners in the camp hear the gunfire and they never see that man again!"

Another horrible example was provided by the army ranger. "I had experienced in different ways how the North treat us. But one I never forget is when they killed a lieutenant colonel, one major, and the first lieutenant by setting a fire to destroy a house where the three people were locked in a stockade with their legs sticking out. They killed our comrades by torturing them until they were dead!"

For the F-5 pilot, the execution of one escapee became very personal. He learned that his half-brother had attempted escape and been recaptured and executed.

The death of the escapee did not end his punishment. The North Vietnamese had further trials in store for his spirit when the body was interred in an unmarked grave. In the Vietnamese culture, to be buried this way damned the deceased's spirit to wander eternally. To leave the grave unmarked was also a powerful insult to the prisoner's family because they would not be able to visit the site.

The A-37 pilot was the voice of rage for all the prisoners regarding this practice. "Yes, you know the Communists are very, very inhumane. You are alive. They can punish you, anything, but when you die they won't inform your family. They bury the body in the forest too. When the prisoner dies, we write down his name. One day we have to cover the top—buffalo, you know. We don't know who is buried where!"

The air force administrator described a somber and sad final task. "Many prisoners were dead. Their bodies were wrapped in rush mats, no coffins, and buried by friends in silence at night."

While execution was in store for the recaptured prisoner, there was also a price to be paid by his barrack mates. The young company commander explained further. "Anytime one prisoner escaped, they beat the comrades that lie beside the escaped man."

A very cruel form of punishment was isolation in the conex, a large steel case that originally contained United States Army supplies, but which the Communists adapted for punishment. The physician commented on the physical deprivation of this punishment. "What we call the conex. No daylight, nothing!"

Without food or water, in darkness, and subjected to searing daytime temperatures, the prisoner, unless released, died hideously. His cries for mercy could be heard by the other prisoners. Later in the northern camps, the returned captive was severely punished by isolation but was not allowed to die. After release from the isolation, the prisoner was moved to another camp. Punishment by isolation tested the prisoner's survival skills as no other aspect of his incarceration did.

The company commander described the punishments: "In one camp, they have a room they call the discipline room. In that room, the prisoner lived in a narrow box. He cannot stand, but he cannot lay down. They cut the meals. Every day they just have one meal. Anytime a prisoner was released from the discipline room, he cannot walk for at least one week after that."

The battalion commander described what he witnessed. "They beat the prisoners for a while, and they cuff the leg and the hand and leave them there for three days or more. They were thrown in the hole . . . they are in the hole."

Additionally, they defecated in the hole. The regimental commander spent an extraordinary length of time, five years, in isolation. By necessity, he learned coping techniques to keep his emotions under control.

"While serving time in solitary confinement. I had to speak out to defuse my angry temper. I learned that If I spoke by mistake—a complaint, for example—I would have been punished by the guards. Therefore, I just sang the 'blue songs.' I strongly believed that singing was a way to relax. Singing lifted my morale and spirit."

In his darkest hour, when singing failed, this man found another way to sustain himself. "As long as you could hear other prisoners, you could endure."

QUANG HONG MAC (RAPHAEL M.V. MAC)

The air force pilot recounted what it took to be released from isolation. "The length of time in isolation was determined by the supposed sincerity of the repentance. If you write a report and say, 'I am guilty, I am back now, and I won't do it again,' they release you."

Chapter 6

The Journey Inward

The Journey Inward

When the hope for repatriation after three years in the camps was dashed by the Communists, the prisoners were forced to face a brutal truth. The maintenance man put it bluntly. "They said, 'Well, concentration for reeducation has no time limit.' That's the problem. No time limit!"

The former F-5 pilot expressed that reality in another way. "I tried to have a reality check. I don't have any country. I don't have any family. I don't have anything."

And so, the prisoners turned inward to find wellsprings of survival. The prisoner's culture provided such an inner source. The policeman was the spokesperson for many prisoners. "In any situation, be patient. You have to be patient."

The physician became "calm, submissive, and flexible." The air force administrator drew on another Vietnamese trait. "The Vietnamese people, we have strength of will, you know."

Some prisoners, like the air force administrator, relied somewhat on superstition for hope. "I tell you about superstition. You know superstition. If you have twelve camp, you be released. I had twelve."

The policeman developed an extrasensory perception of the future. "Sometimes I have a sixth sense. I feel something will happen to me."

Many Catholics found solace in religion. The policeman put his faith unequivocally in God. "I had a strong belief that I would not die when I was in the prison camp."

The Catholic priest saw his cell as a "penance house." The F-5 pilot related why he prayed. "You don't have any other resources. One prayer a day, like a pater."

For some Buddhist prisoners, religion also offered solace. The maintenance officer prayed to Buddha "to save my life and help me increase the energy and will to endure hardships in the prison."

For others, like the helicopter pilot, Buddhism was no help. "I am a Buddhist, but I am not a practicing Buddhist. The religions always say, 'Do good things,' but say, 'Kill people.' The war killed the good things of my Buddhist theory for me!"

For some prisoners, the inward journey became a time of reflection on one's self. The army ranger reported that he learned a lot about himself. The priest used the time to "think on my life and my activities." Other officers penetrated deep into their psyches and discovered a sustaining core belief.

The regimental commander followed his inward path. "I think that I can survive. I never thought about committing suicide, even in the cell. I had to survive!"

Hope could be a powerful inner force. The A-37 pilot used that power. "One day I hoped I will leave prison. My hope made me feel good."

The regimental commander also drew on hope. "I am an optimist. I hoped for a better future." He also reframed his situation. "I think maybe if I were in combat I would be killed. Here, I am still alive. That cheered me up!"

Some prisoners hoped that a perfidious ally would return. The company commander hoped that "Americans help us."

Other prisoners looked for hopeful signs in unlikely places. The policeman was such a man. "I have some hope again when they tell us to fill out our form, like a history form, with first name first and last name last. That is irregular. That is not normally the Vietnamese paperwork, but we felt that was like American paperwork."

The F-5 pilot was more practical. "First you have to really see what you have, what you can do. Do not use emotions, because you will have payback, get consequences."

Assailed continually with multiple horrors, just reframing thoughts would not suffice for the prisoner. The air force administrator described how he dealt with the inhumanity that surrounded him. "When we go out to work, we meet some people. They move from their camp to the other camp; you know, to receive the manioc. You can talk about the conditions. 'Oh, Mr. Lei is dead.' or 'Mr. Mei is dead.' I keep it all inside."

Instead, the prisoner, by necessity, had to follow his inward path to a safer emotional ground. Such a safe place was indifference. The maintenance officer found that state of mind through his cultural heritage. "If you want to survive, you must become indifferent to everything, be resigned to your fate."

The air force pilot achieved the same state. "I accept fate and am peaceful." An alternative was to become, as the helicopter pilot stated, "just like a machine."

However, going within oneself could be dangerous for the prisoner if he could not achieve an emotional state of indifference or an acceptance of fate. The physician described what could occur instead. "They torture you mentally. It's more than physical. They don't beat you. They don't handcuff you. They don't kick you, but they torture you in your mind!" The physician became someone he didn't know. "Actually, I was scared, because I don't feel like myself before the reeducation."

There was another dangerous emotional state, depression, which was as debilitating as hunger. The army ranger described the state of his mind at times. "When you think about what is happening, it makes you depressed. Day after day, a thousand bamboo will be cut down, and you imagine what tomorrow will bring. Everything makes you depressed."

The A-37 pilot, himself very depressed at times, related where depression could lead. "Sometimes bad psychology. They think too much about family. They worry, but they can do nothing, so they get very depressed. Depression can kill them easy!"

Experiencing unremitting depression, it was only a matter of time until the prisoner gave up hope. For those prisoners who could not escape from that bleak emptiness, death came rather swiftly. Such men usually stopped eating and within several days died.

The company commander described through an interpreter his thoughts of giving up hope. "After two years, he knew he would live the rest of his life in a prison camp."

The air force pilot released his wife from their marriage. "I sent her back a letter. I don't know when I will see you and the kids, so you are free." She later divorced him.

The regimental commander also plumbed the depths of despair. "While I was in the cell, I asked the guard to give me some medicine. He says no, so I say, 'You kill me!' I opened my shirt and say, 'Kill me!' He went out and bring back some medicine for me, and I calm down and come back to my cell. Too painful. I was frustrated and had no hope left."

Each man in his own way struggled back from depression. The air force administrator had a method to raise his depressed spirits. "When I am depressed, I walked in the forest. I am a survivor."

The army ranger also waged war against his depressed state. "You think about how to survive, and then you have to think what is good for you."

The F-5 pilot played mind games. "I devised in my mind every day the unique experience that I had lived in US."

Near Death

For the majority of the prisoners, there came a time when the capriciousness of their existence brought them face to face with death. In those intimate moments, what did each man draw on to survive? The air force administrator faced imminent death due to starvation, but survived with the help of comrades:

> *One time I think I die. That time, I was very, very debilitated. I weighed about ninety-five pounds. One afternoon when I come back from the field, after receiving a bowl of food for horses, feed grain, after I set up my bowl, I said, "I don't know." I felt so bad. I fell over. I became unconscious.*
>
> *They put me on my bed. I come alive, and I ask them, "Why I am here?"*
>
> *"We thought you dead!"*
>
> *I am very lucky. They used petroleum, doing a massage to save my life.*

The pilot faced death during his escape from the camp and believed he was saved by a miraculous power:

> *In one escape, I was swimming across a lake, two of us towing three prisoners who could not swim. I was getting very tired.*

41

My arms and legs were cramping. I vomited into the lake. I thought I was going to die. I thought it was the end. I cleared my mind and prayed to God for help.

"Please, if I am still alive, just show me the way to go."

It was a miracle! An arm pointed in the direction I was supposed to swim.

The politician faced death in a conex and used mind control and willpower to survive:

You know that it is hot in Viet Nam, and they put me in the conex box about one month. I don't wear any clothes. It was very hot inside. We have water. I know the discipline of Kung Fu, and I know what is going on. If you live in a condition like that, you cannot drink much water. You drink too much the sweat will come out, and you will feel pain. I prayed and, using the techniques of Kung Fu, sat on the floor, concentrating to pray and don't think about anything else for rest of the day/nighttime, until I become tired and sleep.

The intelligence officer, suffering from untreated diabetes, was pronounced dead and placed in a mortuary. He was unable to understand how he survived. "Sometimes during my journey in the north, they put me in the mortuary. I was dead at that time, so they put me in the mortuary, waiting for the next morning to bury me. But I don't know what happened during the night. I survived."

The battalion commander faced death, trying to escape from the invading Chinese forces:

"I remember that night when I could hear firing between the Chinese and Vietnamese troops on the border. At midnight they get us up, and we carry our stuff. We move about sixty miles with the heavy stuff on our shoulders, but at that time I had a piece of metal in my joint, the left leg. It was very hard for me at that time, but I don't know what happened. It seemed like a miracle. So one moment it happens that I can walk again.

The maintenance officer had a particularly harrowing experience. "One time—I don't know how to say it—I walk out at dawn or sunset, and suddenly I see nothing. Night blind! I ate a lot of green hot peppers, hoping the vitamin A in them will help."

The Catholic priest became very ill and survived by a combination of treatments. "I got very sick. I was given medication. I got better by exercise. I motivated my body to be active."

Finally, the F-5 pilot related how he nearly poisoned himself to death. "I went to work in the forest, and I saw mushrooms, so I picked them up and cooked them. That night I start to sweat. The cadre came down because they reported to the commandant that they have a sick person. I was in the limbo between life and death. I don't feel any pain or anything. I hear someone in the background say that he is dying."

Quick thinking by other prisoners saved his life. They mixed sugar into hot water along with the medicine, and the F-5 pilot was able to swallow it. He gradually recovered.

Chapter 7

Release from the Reeducation Camp

Beginning in 1982, the North Vietnamese authorities began to release those prisoners who were deemed not to be a threat to the new society. While it heartened the men to see others released, there was also sadness at being left behind. At those times, being in captivity became even harder to bear. The A-37 pilot, imprisoned for ten years, described the disappointment he experienced each time other prisoners were released, and the regimental commander echoed that sentiment. "Every time I saw somebody leave the camp, I was very sad for myself."

The Communist technique for releasing the prisoners was fairly standard throughout the camp system. The prisoner would be held back from his work detail, told to pack his belongings, and then move to another building. Until he left the camp, the prisoner would remain separated from his fellow prisoners. This period of separation could be one night or one week. Through it all, the prisoner did not know if he was to be released or transferred to a new camp. This wait could be an excruciating time for the prisoner.

The F-5 pilot, a nine-year veteran of the camps, related the necessity of keeping control of his emotions while watching others leave the camp. "Usually, the night before Independence Day or Tet, they will say, 'Today we will have these names released.' If you pay too much attention to those kinds of things you will be crazy. I think it will demoralize you more."

The A-37 pilot explained that he dealt with his own uncertainty, whether he was to be released or transferred to another camp, by not thinking about the possibilities. He did not want to be hurt. Some prisoners, like the maintenance officer, an eight-year detainee, had an inkling they would be released. "I think maybe I will be moved, but also that I may be released, because the guard who called me out, he smiled."

The regimental commander, who had been imprisoned for seventeen years, was elated when he heard the news. "The day that it was announced that I was to be released, I tell the guard, 'You know it is time. I go home. You cannot keep me anymore!'"

Upon release, the prisoner was shocked when he saw how different he was from the people outside the camp. The physician, after almost three years in the camp, described his experience. "You changed. You don't know when. Gradually. But I don't know until I was released. That's when I see other people. I know I have changed. Our clothes, we used sandbags to make our clothes."

The air force administrator, after ten years of imprisonment, thanked a god upon his release. "We also stopped at the prison gate, faced back to the prison, and prayed to the hell deity with a good-bye and asked never to be here again."

Finally, the air force pilot, after twelve years of prison, described meeting his wife on the day of his release. "They came from Nha Trang by train to welcome me from the prison. My wife was informed in a dream by two angels aged ten. That's mysterious!"

The Meaning of Captivity

Almost to a man, the former prisoners initially understood the meaning of their captivity to be the revenge or punishment meted out by the victorious North Vietnamese Communists. The military policeman was blunt in his assessment of what imprisonment meant. "I think they were revenging us!"

Many of the men believed they were losers and could expect nothing more. The F-5 pilot understood it that way at the beginning of his captivity. "Probably, I am being punished because I am on the losing side."

For several of the former prisoners, punishment and revenge was what it remains to this day. The company commander expressed that view." Revenge! Even now, revenge!"

However, the meaning of the experience changed for some men, like the A-37 pilot. "I think that at first it was punishment. But as it went longer, I know the reason they keep me in prison was because they want to show the world they are not violent. They don't kill people."

The A-5 pilot's understanding also changed. "I understood the situation when I saw they kept changing the guards every three or six months. The guards said we were contaminating them because they were exposed to a very dangerous element. We were a threat to their regime!"

The air force pilot also believed Communists were trying to protect the society from the prisoner until the prisoner learned "new ways."

For many of the men, whether Buddhist or Catholic, there were deeper layers of meaning for the experience. The priest believed that his incarceration was punishment inflicted by a much greater power than the North Vietnamese Communists. "I believe in God. He punishes me, but he protects me. God will use communism to punish."

The police officer understood the camp experience as a spiritual metaphor. "I am here, and if there is a heaven, reeducation camp will be hell!"

For the F-5 pilot, it was a personal destiny that led him to and through the camps. "I don't have a clear explanation. I think it's fate or destiny. I just let everything go, then things will be better."

For other former prisoners, like the company commander, personal destiny was wrapped in a larger meaning. "I don't think about imprisonment itself, but I think if I am one individual in the whole thing, that it is the end of our country. I think something tied me in that prison. So, the question is why? Because of the country's destiny, the end."

For several of the prisoners, the meaning of the survival represented a passage through a consuming fire to a new existence, one that could not have occurred without the camps. The battalion commander articulated his understanding of that passage. "Yes, there were meanings for the camps. My friends who come to this country before me ask me why I was so happy. I told them, 'When I was in the reeducation camp, I had nothing. In this country, I work so hard for my wife's new clothes. I work for my children's college.'"

The air force pilot saw his reeducation camp experience as a catalyst for a new life. "I was a normal man, but my life was an unordinary one. It blossomed!" Yet, for him the experience remains surreal. "It feels like unreal, like a dream."

The physician took the meaning of reeducation further. For him it was no less than a transformation of the self. "I have to transform myself from the bad guy to a good guy to be released back to the new society."

The air force maintenance officer drew from his experience that he had the duty to tell the younger generation of his experiences. "Pass my knowledge, my experience about Communism onto the next young generation. Never trust in what they say! Lost generation, very sad."

For all of these men and their families, their struggles to achieve personal freedom continued after their release from the camps. Most were placed under house arrest for varying periods of time. Some attempted escape more than once before they succeeded. All of them left family members behind in Viet Nam. No matter what the hardship, the men were sustained by what they had endured and overcome. They had paid a high price for freedom, and they had become stronger for it.

The battalion commander eloquently spoke for the rest of them. "After many years of working hard, living in the worst conditions, right now I believe that I am stronger. The value of each person, that's all that matters. Not from the diploma, but from the strength inside."

Epilogue

The Major Strategies of China Collapsed
By Hoa Truong
(Originally appeared on thedawnmedia.com, December 25, 2019)

China's communist regime represents the ape herd, as its great master Karl Marx promoted, and Mao Tse Tung accepted the scam's history about the original human. After the Second World War, China emerged as the global thug, and with the Soviet-Union created the Cold War. The Indochina War was commanded by China, and in the Điện Biên Phủ battle, the untrained four-star General Võ Nguyên Giáp was a puppet. The hot spot that was the Viet Nam War proved the deep involvement of China's communist regime as it sent hundreds of thousands of troops to fight alongside with North Viet Nam's communists. The left media and the prominent Vietcong's supporters, like Jane Fonda, John Kerry, Joe Biden, Bill and Hillary Clinton, and the others have never told the truth about China and the Soviet Union, plus the Global Communist Bloc provided weapons and troops to help the Hanoi regime carry out the so-called fighting against the Empire American. Indeed, after the Geneva Conference signed on July 20, 1954, North Viet Nam's communist regime obeyed the orders from its great master China and the Soviet Union to create the war, so on May 1959, despite the US Army and allies who didn't come to South Viet Nam (the first US troop just came to South Viet Nam from 1965), therefore, Hồ Chí Minh launched the campaign: "fighting against Empire American," and Hồ Chí Minh ordered Major General Bùi Xuân Đăng to found the Special Task Force, code 559, to gather 100,000 laborers to prepare the abandoned road linking Viet Nam-Laos-Cambodia, the Hồ Chí Minh Trail. The former member of the People's Liberation Army Xiao- Bing Li wrote *The Dragon in the Jungle*, in which he revealed that China sent more than 430,000 troops to Indochina from 1968 to 1973 (when the Paris Peace Accords were signed). After the Soviet Union and the Eastern European communist Bloc collapsed in the early 1990s, China gathered the vestiges of communist countries in Asia, the Cold War transformed into the Cool War, but communism's character never changed. China and its vassal Viet Nam have applied the lizard changes the color's skin tactic to cheat the West with the economic pattern "the free market is led by socialism."

After the historic visit of US President Richard Nixon in 1972, China joined the free market and later the WTO, and the world has been complicated by China's communist regime. The appearance of China in the free market and the international community is like Satan or evil infiltrating heaven. The largest communist regime has conspired a global hegemonic strategy, and the rapaciousness of China has been carried out by a soft army that has attacked the counterparts through global economic terror. The trade trap, government trap, and the debt trap help China colonize countries involved in economically with China. Beijing used the money to buy foreign assets, including prime ministers, presidents, ministers, and powerful officials. President Bill Clinton led the US as an actual henchman of China in the White House.

President Bill Clinton helped China grew faster with the Most Favored Nation policy and the hoax of climate change to curb Western industry while China freely releases carbon dioxide and sells solar power. Nowadays, the hoax of climate change is a vestige of Bill Clinton and Al Gore and creates disorder in the West with the Green Guard (a form of the Red Guard of Mao Tse Tung in the Culture Revolution), the Extinction Rebellion, Vegan.

The dangerous invasion of China threatens the world, China conspires to topple the US and control the world by communism (Maoist). The first Muslim and communist President Barrack Obama performed the global hegemonic strategy of Beijing. President Barrack Obama flagged China when it built and militarized the illegally artificial islands in disputed waters. China used the money to carry out the plan of one belt and one road. The money comes from the scam's business and stolen technology. China's growth comes from Western loss.

China and Democrats in the US plan to control the world in 2025. The brazen pride of China appeared in foreign policy by intimidating counterparts and snubbing the US. China does want Hillary Clinton to becomes the first female US president. She will continue to carry out the job of Bill Clinton (if Hillary becomes the US president, Bill Clinton will advise his wife to drive the US into China's vassal and the greedy monetary couple will earn a lot of money). Unfortunately, the US people elected President Donald Trump, so the major strategies of China collapsed. Democrats and China didn't surmise the appearance of Donald Trump. China and Democrats maximally pushed the propaganda in the presidential campaign in 2016. The left media launched the psychological warfare campaign with the formula 3F (False poll + Fake News + Fabricated story) to mislead the public and influence undecided voters. The propaganda became the paranoia of Hillary Clinton, the false polls always showing Hillary Clinton advanced over Donald Trump by at least four points, while some polls confirmed twelve points. Hillary Clinton absolutely believed her dream would come true and she became arrogant in the debates. She claimed Donald Trump unfit to be the commander in chief. Unfortunately, the night of November 8, 2016, transformed the wonderful dream of Hillary Clinton to a nightmare. China fell into panic after President Donald Trump was elected. President Donald Trump cracked down on the major strategies of China, so China's plan to control the world in 2025 was nullified by the trade war, which is like the war to fight against terrorists.

The global economic terror of China has struck the world from the first visit to Beijing of President Richard Nixon in 1972. China joined the free market and later the WTO. The global economic terror is more dangerous than the Islamic State or any other terror organization. China has used the soft army to invade the world by the trade trap, government trap, and the debt trap. China has used its economy and finance to colonize the counterparts. The West, including the US, are the main targets. President Donald Trump becomes the disaster for China's communists, and Democrats see the White House's swamp to be drained out, with the felons, corruption, and treason of the Democratic. The major strategies of China collapsed:

1. The spy network ruined:

* The Western alerts to China's overseas students carrying out the spy mission, with stolen technology and intoxicating the young generations in university. When the espionage agent is debunked, the spy mission loses its mission.
* The West warns China's business and financial agents from exploiting the business investments to carry out the spy mission and influence politics.
* The well-known cyber spy 61389 unit of the People's Liberation Army lost some of its effectiveness when the world recognized the enemy.

2-The offshore economy and market loss:

* Huawei is banned, and the giant telecommunication company owned by the People's Liberation Army loses business and its cyber spy mission.
* The financial system is on the brink of collapse after economic losses, and the US tariffs cause damage.
* China lost the consumer's trust through poor quality products, contamination, poison, and short life. Those facts worsen China's economy when the global consumer boycotts China's products

3-The domestic battle decides the fate of China's communist regime.

* The mountain of debt was $USD 40 trillion in 2017, and now, the debt escalates, it should be $USD 45 or 50 trillion. China's debt amounted to 15 percent of total world debt., and the IMF warned of China's inability to pay it. The economic war crippled China, and the totalitarian regime is at risk. China must take more than fifty years to pay the debt if its economy is like the US.
* China's currency devalued at least 5 percent, and it surpassed the alert level of one USD equals seven yuan. The decline in the value of the yuan causes inflation without control in the mainland.
* Massive joblessness is the real threat to the Red dynasty. The ape regime faces the abhorrence of Chinese people after more than seventy years of rule by terror and propaganda.

The economic plan of one belt and one road is ruined, and the illegal islands built in disputed waters faces the difficulty of overrunning costs . China flinches to quell the democratic movement in Hong Kong that proved the failure of Beijing. The Hong Kong Human Rights and Democracy Act 2019 (HKHRDA) issued by the US forced China to withdraw the plan to create a second Tiananmen Square in Hong Kong.

The panic and the potential loss of China reflect the unconditional impeachment of President Donald Trump. On the other hand, China does want to stop the economic war, so Beijing silently endorses the comrade Democrats to carry out the unconstitutional impeachment, therefore, the bush law cannot recognize in the US Constitution, actually the Senate. The people believe China stands behind the maniac impeachment. Probably, Beijing indirectly intervenes in US politics by using comrade Democrats to impeach President Donald Trump. Certainly, China loses nothing when the cheat impeachment failed, but Democrats to be sacrificed by China's interest. If Democrats succeeded with the scam's impeachment, China just spends a little money and privileges and Beijing will get the facilities, the best policies granted by the henchmen.

The major strategies of China collapsed to trash Democrats, both must receive the dire consequences, China's dream turns into a nightmare and Democrats fear the While House's swamp drains out.

China is the Professional Burglar on the Planet
By Hoa Truong
(Originally appeared on thedawnmedia.com on December 29, 2019)

After joining the free market and WTO, the largest communist country appeared the real face of a rogue state. The world identified China as a den of thieves, the hub of counterfeit and the center of a cheat, the bush law, and the totalitarian regime couldn't accord the international community. The appearance of China in the free market is like a gang officially operates in society. The US and democratic countries developed without China before the sanctions lifted.

China's growth comes from dishonest methods. The clever and professional burglar is the giant with the foot of clay also became the current member of the UN's Security Council and has the diplomatic system worldwide. Certainly, the thieves are criminals. There is no school, university, or college to teach the burglary career. Therefore, communism and socialism is the place for teaching burglary.

The communist paradise of Karl Marx, Maoist, Hồ Chi Minh's thoughts and the others are the paradise of burglary. The pauperization's policy of communism or socialism originates from the social problem, the poor people without support from the government, they become the casual burglars. In the communist paradise, the thieves can steal anything, including the excrement, because the human release provides the fertilizer. In Viet Nam, Hồ Chí Minh defines the excrement as a precious asset, the nation wide's economic development called Uncle Ho's Fish Pond helped the family solve the toilet and also feeding a kind of fish called" Cá Vồ" does love human excrement. The Fish Vồ processes the Ba-Sa fillet and exports to the West to make money. The phrase, "The free market is led by socialism" has been applied in China and Viet Nam. The lizard changes skin color tactic has deceived the innocent politicians in the West and naïve national leaders.

In the paradise of burglary in communist countries like Viet Nam, the people always watch the thieves, saying: "socialism means the toilet mud fence" that reflects the outstanding of communism and Hồ Chí Minh's thoughts. The Western and democratic countries concern the human excrement is the wasted materials, actually, the hygiene's concern. Therefore, the communist countries have used the excrement into economic development. In Viet Nam, Hanoi's suburb has the excrement market at Cổ Nhuễ's village (someone created the fake excrement for sale and the local government arrested). In a communist country like Viet Nam, even the excrement can make the fake, so the communist paradise couldn't trust. The Vietcong's supporters like Jane Fonda (Hanoi Jane) concealed the excrement market and the cruelty of North Viet Nam's regime in the Viet Nam War. The sibling of the communist is the left media, the left journalists, the left reporters who release the fake news, it is the character of Karl Marx's pupils.

The people who live in the communist paradise recognize the agricultural products are of poor quality, with poison, contamination, and hygienic concern, so the agricultural products of the West are favored by the Chinese people in the mainland. It causes China to fail to impose retaliatory tariffs on the US's agricultural products, as China's tariffs hit back at Chinese people.

The model of socialism in Viet Nam exposes the multiple forms of burglary as dog thieves, cat thieves, log thieves, soil thieves, and other burglaries. The professional thieves and casual burglars snoop everywhere in the communist paradise, so the foreign tourists must be careful while visiting Viet Nam and China. The legal burglars are communists, actually, the high-ranking cadres stole the people's sweat, and they become the millionaires and billionaires. The stolen money was deposited at Western banks and used to purchase assets at the capitalist countries.

China is the great master of Vietcong's regime, so China is professional burglary at a high level. China has arrayed the global burglary system that carries out into multiple forms and malicious methods. The stolen technology is a vital tactic. China also stole the trademark of Western brands. The foreign factories in China are the victims of the stolen trademarks plus technology. Therefore, they couldn't take legal action because China has never respected the law, but the bush law can apply to the legal argument. China makes a profit from the loss of the West, and the money comes from the burglary using the money for the global hegemonic strategy.

The den of thieves illegally built and militarized the artificial islands in disputed waters, the sand provided by Viet Nam, a vassal of China. The debt trap is a high level of invasion or the clever burglary from the lands of counterparts. The growth of China is like the Nazis in the Second World War. The global hegemonic ambition of the giant burglar has never stopped. China has stolen the fish in disputed waters and also stole the soil of Philippine territories. The cargo ships of China stole the soil of Davao Del Notre Province of the Philippines, the position located at the West Philippine sea or the Spratly islands. The Philippines won in the International Court; the artificial islands of China are illegal, therefore, Beijing ignores international law, including its neighbor countries by its brazen and aggressive attitude. The world watches the global burglar and the cunning conqueror using the soft army to colonize the counterparts by the trade ties and free trade agreements.

The Cost of Unconstitutional Impeachment
By Hoa Truong
(Originally appeared on thedawnmedia.com on January 1, 2020)

The desperate impeachment hits back at Democrats and trashed the hidden communist party in the US. It was the greatest witch hunt in US history when the Democratic lawmakers ignored

57

the Constitution, instead, they applied the bush law plus the underworld rules of Congress. It shows the death of Democrats is underway when the US people recognized the real face of a political party founded on January 8, 1828, by Andrew Jackson and Martin Van Buren. The demagogic policies couldn't cover the betrayal, corruption and the treason of the prominent high profiles as Bill Clinton, Barrack Obama, Joe Biden, Hillary Clinton, John Kerry and, others. The current leaders of Democrats in Congress and the Senate helped the US people realize the shadow of its party. The arrogance and greedy power of Nancy Pelosi become the disaster of Democrats.

The taxpayers wasted tens of millions of US dollars on the dirty political game of the Democratic party. The Democratic representatives have stormed the Congress after the midterm elections of 2018. The lawmakers turned into terrorists to attack President Donald Trump by the cunning tactics to impeach with the fabricated dossiers, the designed witnesses, plus the hidden whistleblowers. The US taxpayers to be exploited by the terror mission of lawmaker terrorist leader Nancy Pelosi and her assistants are Adam Schiff with Jerry Nadler.

The unconstitutional impeachment pushes Democrats into peril, actually, the US people's abhorrence will contribute to the landslide victory of President Donald Trump and Republicans in the elections of 2020. Democrats have fallen in love with the corruption and treason, so the quagmire of impeachment worsens the situation when the efforts to remove President Donald Trump failed. The concerned Democrats recognize the dirty political game of their leaders conflict the national interest and the people that cause Democrats to lose the support from the grassroots.

The US people and the concerned Democratic supporters know its party trashed by the greedy power's woman Nancy

Pelosi and her actual assistants to launch the scam's impeachment against President Donald Trump. The Liberal Harvard law professor Alan Dershowitz slammed House Speaker Nancy Pelosi who withholds two articles for impeachment without a reason and conflicts the Constitution. The obstinate attitude of Nancy Pelosi abuses the power and obstructs the Congress. Moreover, Nancy Pelosi wants to command the Senate, it is so funny and impossible. Law professor Alan Dershowitz said: "It is wrong constitutionally, and it is wrong morally, and it is wrong politically. And it's wrong for America, in our view."

Democrats are losing support from the US people and their party. After Democratic House Representative Jeff Van Drew officially declared to join Republicans in December 2019, four Democratic Senators, Jack Layton of Michigan, Christina Clark of Washington, Gordon Campbell of California, and Kareem Jabari of New York, have abandoned their party because the Democratic Congress illegally acted against the US president.

Democrats have fallen into the internal disorder and will lose the election in 2020. The impeachment is like a toy playing by the adult that shows the Donkey's Head Party snubs democracy. President Donald Trump twittered: "Nancy is a liar and a fraud. We just witnessed the most PARTISAN SCAM in American history and it resulted in the house officially IMPEACHING me. My team is sending me a list of everyone who does their part and donates before MIDNIGHT. I need you on my side in this Impeachment Fight!"

President Donald Trump can file the lawsuit against Nancy Pelosi who defamed the US president plus the compensation. The Justice Department can prosecute Nancy Pelosi, Adam Schiff, and Jerry Nadler. They cheated the Constitution, they used fake documents, and designed witnesses to impeach and treason.

The Psychological Warfare Repeats in the 2020 Election

By Hoa Truong
Originally appeared on thedawnmedia.com on January 1, 2020)

In 2016, during the candidate's nomination of Republicans, there was a group of 370 prominent economists, including eight Nobel Laureates, who signed a letter warning Republicans about candidate Donald Trump as "a dangerous, destructive choice for the country." But candidate Donald Trump defeated sixteen heavyweight Republican politicians, and he transformed the wonderful dream of former Senator Hillary Clinton to a nightmare. Certainly, the top economic academics couldn't influence Republicans to choose a presidential candidate. Nowadays, dishonest academics and scholars exploit the doctoral degree to serve individual favor or the political purpose. They humiliate the intellectual line and damage the prestige of universities.

All the dire warnings of 370 top economists in the US turned to garbage after President Donald Trump entered office on January 20, 2017. The well-known economists, including eight Nobel Prize winners, succeeded the economic doctors, but they distorted the career and became the ECONOMIC DOCTORS. Probably, eight Nobel Prize in economics winners should be awarded the Confucius Peace Prize made in China because of their stance and action responds to China's global economic terror. Moreover, in the campaign, candidate Donald Trump accused China bullied the US's economy with unfair trade. In the passage of time, the Confucius Peace Prize awarded Lien Chan in 2010, Vladimir Putin in 2011, Kofi Anna and Yuan Longping in 2012, Yicheng in 2013, Fidel Castro in 2014, Robert Mugabe in 2015, Shen Liangliang in 2016, Hun Sen in 2017.

President Donald Trump makes America great again, and economic growth faster. The era of SATAN's Barrack Obama obsesses the US people, but the food stamp period is over and now, the SANTA's era of the US with the potential Commander in Chief and the Great Economic General brings back the strength of the United States of America. The great achievements of President Donald Trump become the hatred of Democrats, China's fear, and other enemies frightened. President Donald Trump makes the unemployment rate hit the lowest record since 1969. The Dow Jones reached 28,461 on December 30, 2019, comparing the era of Barrack Obama, Dow Jones struggled under 17,000. President Donald Trump makes wages rise, jobs rise, and the stock market rise. However, the left media and Democrats mislead the public about the US's economy while the economic war with China is occurring. The concealment is no longer. The high technological communication with multiple information sources plus the social media defeats the media cheat.

The basic economy's lesson warns the economic crisis when the stock market tumbled, the jobless increased, the currency devalued. Therefore, those facts have not appeared in the US, instead, China has the conditions to conduct the economic disaster. Nevertheless, China thinks the second term of President Donald Trump will be inevitable, actually, the landslide victory is waiting for Republicans. Democrats frighten the White House's swamp is underway to drain out, so China and "comrade Democrats" do want to prevent the second term of President Donald Trump to ease the tariffs and Democratic high profiles will escape the serious crimes, corruption, and treason. The unconstitutional impeachment reflects the extreme fear of China and Democrats, its reason rushes Democrats to sacrifice its party's prestige and future to launch the desperate impeachment.

The scam's impeachment failed when the Senate, controlled by Republicans, so Democrats and China have fallen into a hopeless status. The disaster is waiting for their fate, the incident of old tactic repeats as 370 economists cheated in the election 2016. On December 30, 2019, the boss of Amazon, Jeff Bezos, frightened investors by his dire statement: "I predict one day, Amazon will fail." Mr. Jeff Bezos warns bankruptcy will have happened. The US people have no surprise about Amazon's boss, Jeff Bezos, who purchased the prominent fake news *The Washington Post* in 2013 for $US 250 million in cash. So, Mr. Jeff Bezos launches the scare campaign to undermine the second term of President Donald Trump. Therefore, Mr. Jeff Bezos cannot compare the professionals with 370 economists including eight Nobel Prize of economic winners, actually, he is a businesslike Donald Trump. Moreover, The Bank of America raises the alarm about 2020 will be the end of globalization and the social disruption. However, someone in the Bank of America cannot tell something about the outcome of the global economy in 2020 while the World Bank and IMF have not released a statement to the world. China should pay someone in The Bank of America to appeal to the US people, it is the phony psychological warfare.

The market researchers believe the technology favors the economy is worth more than $US 19 trillion. Therefore, China has lacked technology, nevertheless, the stolen tactic is prevented by the ban of Huawei and the world alerts the cyber spy unit 61389 of the People's Liberation Army also owned Huawei, certainly, China worries about technological growth. The intimidation carries out by the psychological warfare of Amazon's boss and The Bank of America has not convinced the US people, but the victim's countries of China's trade trap being panicked when the banking system of China is on the brink of collapse and the economic peril conducts their economy following China.

The Sclerosis Character of Economic Socialism
By Hoa Truong
(Originally appeared on thedawnmedia.com on January 3, 2020)

In the Cold War, the Global Communist Bloc applied the propaganda forwarding the technology, and the weapon advanced the US to bluff the world. Indeed, the Soviet Union failed the arms race with the US, actually, the Star War Program (Strategic Defense Initiative) promoted by President Ronald Reagan on March 23, 1983, that ruined the developed missile of the cradle of Global Communist Bloc. Nevertheless, after the Soviet Union collapsed, the world knew well the propaganda of communist reflects a saying: "do not listen to what the communist says, let's watch what the communist does." Actually, the demagogic propaganda praised the communist paradise to deceive the innocent people and the lazy thinking of the lacking knowledge of inexpert communism's academics in the West.

The books of Karl Marx are like a beautiful cloth covering a garbage bin. The naive Western people have been attracted by the utopian theory, they have become the craziness to believe communism and socialism can create the best society. Indeed, communism that causes the death of more than 100 million people and a billion people enslaved.

The Marxism-Leninist's paranoid get lost the mind despite they knew the communism born the regimes in Soviet-Union, China, Viet Nam, Cambodia (Khmer Rouge), Cuba and the others. On the other hand, the socialists in Western are the hypocritical component, they often raise the mouthful condemnation of the dictatorial regimes, actually, the human rights violation currently occurs in the communist countries. Therefore, they adore and follow socialism that derived from communism, actually, Karl Marx is the mastermind of communism. The fake moral person opposes the crimes, gang but adores Mafia, it is a farce of the socialists in the Western countries.

Communism is the most disastrous development to humanity on the planet. Marxism-Leninist has intoxicated the people since Lenin succeeded in the Ape Revolution in October 1917. The communists lost the human mind, instead of the animal instinct, so the communists pride the genocide, robbery, they have enjoyed the serious crimes that titled the revolution. The communist regimes have eradicated human history from the grassroots and destroyed society. The mind purge covered under the languages of class struggle, social reform, communist paradise, and many nice titles brainwashed its people, even the hell of prison called reeducation. The anti-communist experts' quote: "when a communist is born, obviously, a midwife sees the mouth."

Communism is the enemy of human development. In China, Viet Nam, the Soviet Union, and the other communist regimes eliminated the wealthy component, abolished the intellectuals. Viet Nam Communists carried out the bloody campaign called Landlord Reform. Hồ Chí Minh and propaganda machine launched the slogan: "uproot the intellectual, wealthy, landlord components." China did the same policy, so after communists controlled the country, the illiterate peasants and the low-educated members replaced the intellectuals. Moreover, the education of the communist regime applies the rule: "family history wins over talent." The Communist regime eliminated the talent, but the regime prioritizes for their children in the education, actually, the overseas study always deserves for the communist members. The intellectuals and academics are the red seeds of the communist regime, they lack the talent and invention.

Socialism is a prime stage of communism, unfortunately, Marxism-Leninist rotted from the fundamental base, so socialism commits suicide the communist regimes and the lagging technology comes from lost democracy. The free speech comes to the freedom that conducts the mind's development and encouraging invention. The sclerosis character of socialism hit back the communist regime on the economy:

* The financial system tied by government, so the people including the communist members distrust the banks, they deposit the money to the "counter-revolution banks" in the West, even Hong Kong.
* The products affected socialism with the untold rule is "negligent work but the best report." The products made from the communist countries, including the Soviet Union, Eastern Europe communist Bloc, all products couldn't compare with the US and European countries (democratic states).
* The people who live in communist regimes lose freedom and the patriotic concern is led by socialism, the scam spirit deeply destroyed the people's invention. The mind contributes to the invention of and national spirit. Unfortunately, socialism framed the patriotism and brainwashed the people's mind. The vital motive of national development to be murdered by socialism and communism.

Despite that the Soviet-Union changed the communist regime from the early 1990s, the toxic communism still remains in Russia. Nowadays, Russia's car cannot compare with German cars, the US, even Japan with Toyota and South Korea has Hyundai.

China has faced the lacking of invention, and Beijing solved the problem by steeling technology, so China becomes the den of thieves, the hub of counterfeit, and the center of a cheat. After more than seventy years, China's communist party built the regime from bloodshed, demagogic policy, propaganda, and terror. China's products worsen the quality, poison, contamination, and short life. However, the poor-quality products of China inundated the global market that was promoted by the innocent leaders and the profit lover's business. The naïve traitors helped China's growth, and nowadays China uses the money to carry out its hegemonic ambition. Unfortunately, sclerosis character hampered the invention, actually, the stolen technology on the space race, the arms race that conducts China into failure. In the Cold War, Soviet Union failed the arms race with the US. Nowadays, China cannot fight with the copied military technology. The aircraft carriers made in China but copied from Ukraine (the old model of the Cold War), so China has sunk into the quagmire of the Chinese dream. The nightmare is coming while the US fights against the global economic terror, China loses the major battles on the economy, finance, the potential damages to be recognized by China's currency devalued.

China should hire "the comrade" left media to propagate fake news and fabricated stories about the unbelievable developments of China's economy, like Chinese scientists made a pig that weighed more than 500 kilograms. China made a laser weapon of military strength. Therefore, the high technological communication era, the multiple information sources, and social media defeat fake news, so China also loses the psychological warfare in the West. Every time the left media and the inexpert academics praise China's strength, actually, the concealment of loss in the economic battle with the US, the disgraced propaganda debunked promptly after the fake news was released. The sclerosis character of socialism has pulled Chinese people in the mainland lagging behind Taiwan, Hong Kong, and Singapore.

Its reason urges Hong Kong people to reject socialism after the territory wrongly handed over to the robber in the mainland.

Chinese people need to abolish socialism in the mainland, the utopian theory labeled Marxism-Leninist and renamed in China is Maoist, in Viet Nam called Hồ Chí Minh's thoughts. Let's compare the living condition between South and North Korea, West and East Germany, actually, South Viet Nam and North Viet Nam. After winning the unpredictable war on April 30, 1975, the former overseas students of North Viet Nam studied in the Soviet Union, East Germany confirmed by a saying: "one year in East Germany equals three years in Soviet Union but a moment at Saigon."

Nowadays, the Vietcong regime continues to pauperize its people and the high profiles of the Viet Nam Communist Party become the millionaire and billionaires, they sent the corrupted money to the West, purchased the assets and sent their red seeds to Western countries. The most counter-revolution countries like the US becomes the dreamland of Viet Nam communist's descendants and their family. Even the communist rejects their communist paradise, unfortunately, in Western countries, the left parties and innocent people still favor socialism as Senator Bernie Sanders and the high profiles of the Democratic Party. The US people and the world knew the fallen communist paradise in Venezuela that shattered and pauperized the country by the crazy idea of Hugo Chavez and Nicolas Maduro. Socialism and communism formulates 3D's= Deception+ Demagogy+ Destruction, so when the left parties like the Australian Labor Party ruled Down Under by Prime Minister Bob Hawke from 1983 to 1991 and Prime Minister Paul Keating from 1991 to 1996, Australia's debt was $AU 96 billion and Prime Minister Kevin Rudd with Prime Minister Julia Gillard from 2007 to 2013, they spent $AU 42 billion of the surplus left by Prime

Minister John Howard then the country started to sink down in the deficit.

Iran Failed to Help China to Stray The Target
By Hoa Truong
(Originally appeared on thedawnmedia.com on January 4, 2020)

China is falling into the panic state and rushing the deal with the US while the major battles of economy, finance, offshore market, stock market crippled and Yuan devalued. The situation of China meets a stratagem of its ancient strategist Sun Tzu: "wait at leisure while the enemy labors." Moreover, the tariffs imposed on the US agricultural products that hit Chinese consumers in the mainland; the sword made in China that stabs Chinese.

There are many times Iran has tried to stray the economic battle of China to military conflicts with Iran. So Teheran acts as a vanguard of China to move the crucial battle on the economy into inappropriate conflict. Iran has tried to mislead the US into the other target and helping China to find a way to escape. Unfortunately, the commander in chief Donald Trump cracks down all cunning tactics.

The Islamic Republic of Iran has applied socialism after the bigot cleric, Sayyid Ruhollah Musavi Khomeini, succeeded a coup in 1979. Iran has become the rogue state, the aggressive attitude of Teheran currently creates tension in the region. Actually, Iran often provokes Israel and the US and allies.

The people believe China stands behind the aggression of Iran. In 2019, when China begged to deal with the US, Iran attacked the oil tankers, downed a US drone and struck Saudi Arabia's oil facilities. Therefore, the US and allies knew the trap of the enemy, so they avoided military conflict, and instead the US sanctions Iran.

It doesn't coincide when China and the US start to meet and discuss the tariffs. A US civilian contractor was killed by a rocket shelled on a base near Kirkuk, Iraq. The culprit was Hezbollah, the actual tool of Iran. The US responded by airstrikes at the military base of Iran's support and killed twenty-five soldiers. Teheran incited the people to protest at the US embassy in Iraq, and they wanted to repeat the Benghazi incident. Iran retaliates by using the terrorist attack the US embassy at Baghdad. It is the old tactic of Vietcong in the Viet Nam War. Vietcong attacked the US embassy at Saigon on the Tet Offensive in 1968. The US casualties and injured to be used into the propaganda and the communist undercover activists, the espionage agents, Democrats, and the left media launched the campaign to slam the US troop and government. But they concealed the potential damages of North Viet Nam with more than 100,000 troops barbecued in the crucial battle.

Nowadays, Iran conspires to use the US casualties at the embassy in Baghdad to pressure the US to ease the sanction. Democrats can exploit the casualties to attack President Donald Trump, and China can excite the innocent people to condemn the White House. However, President Donald Trump promptly responds to an urgent situation. The commander in chief deployed 750 soldiers from the 82nd Airborne Division at Fort Bragg, North California, and put 3,000 soldiers on standby. The US embassy also reinforced 100 Marines and two Apache attack helicopters.

The situation is quite different from Benghazi. In 2012 the terrorist attacked for thirteen, hours and Ambassador Christopher Stevens made 600 requests, but President Barrack Obama, Secretary of State Hillary Clinton, and National Adviser Susan Rice didn't respond. Eventually, the terrorists killed four US servants, including Ambassador Christopher Stevens.

Moreover, Ambassador Christopher Stevens was the key witness about President Barrack Obama related to the Islamic State and terrorists in the Middle East. The people believe Ambassador Christopher Stevens should hold the secrets of Obama, who played the double-cross war game by the US taxpayers and the life of the US soldiers, contractors, foreign officials, and the people doubt President Barrack Obama who was the culprit of four deaths in Benghazi, the key witnesses killed. The investigation of Benghazi cost the US taxpayers $US 3.3 million, but the outcome was nothing. The vestiges of Obama arrayed in the Justice Department and the FBI hampered the investigation. The high level of terrorist-controlled White House in eight years, the US is very lucky, so the country still exists. The Vietnamese people learned the bloody lesson about President Nguyễn Văn Thiệu who acted like a double agent. He destroyed the South Viet Nam Army and helped North Viet Nam claim the unpredictable victory within fifty-five days, indeed, the North Viet Nam communist must take more than three years but the victory was uncertain as North Viet Nam Four Star General Văn Tiến Dũng said before launching twenty divisions to attack South Viet Nam in Ho Chí Minh's campaign on March 1975.

The strong force responds to the situation rapidly that stops the terrorist has tried to create the casualty for political purposes of Iran, China, and Democrats. Moreover, Baghdad is the capital of Iraq, its government cannot ignore the attack, certainly, the terrorists cannot gather the big numerous troops, actually, the force at the embassy can fight with a battalion or even a regiment. On Thursday, January 2nd, 2020, the US Army reported the airstrike near the Bagdad Airport that killed two top military commanders involved in terrorism. Major General Qassem Soliemani, commander of Quds Force, and commander

Abu Mahdi al-Muhamdis, who was deputy chief of PMU Mahdi Almuhandes. The commander of the Iranian Revolution Guard Corps Qassem Soliemani was the perpetrator of terror in Washington DC in 2011, the target was a restaurant and Saudi ambassador to the US, therefore, President Barrack Obama just issued the personal sanctions with four Iranian officials.

Iran must pay the high price after the conspiracy carried out as Sun Tzu's stratagem: "make a sound in the east then strike in the west" to help China into the deal with the US. It is a tactic called "talking during fighting" of the communists. The rapid response of President Donald Trump is like one stone killing two birds. While the unconstitutional impeachment is vain and it hits back at Democrats, China panics the deal with the US plus Hong Kong unrest and Iran failed to mislead the economic war between the US and China to the military conflict. Moreover, two top generals killed by airstrike and Iran have faced tough sanctions on the economy. The world welcomes the deaths of two terror commanders, therefore, Speaker of House Nancy Pelosi whines about how she was not notified of the attack in advance. Moreover, Nancy Pelosi slams President Donald Trump for taking a disproportionate hit on terrorists. Certainly, Democrats deeply related to Iran, actually, President Barrack Obama, Secretary of State John Kerry were close friends with Iran.

Free Speech is Not Free to Support Terrorists
By Hoa Truong
(Originally appeared on thedawnmedia.com on January 6, 2020)

The trade ties and free trade agreement limited the conditions signing between the two countries. The free trade agreement has never accepted the free trade, heroin, cocaine, ice, any kind of drug, into the counterpart. Despite the democratic countries respect for freedom, therefore a farmer cannot allow planting marijuana and the trees banned by the agriculture department, a super market cannot sell the drugs, a media company cannot advertise Mafia, gang, cartel, and drugs, actually, the terror organizations like Al Qaeda, Hamas, Hezbollah, Islamic State ban to advertise and broadcast the endorsement. In the war, the media companies face treason if they exploit the free speech to propagate for the enemy. In the First and Second World Wars, the Western media respected free speech and their countries, so they didn't propagandize for the enemy, actually Nazi and praised leader Adolf Hitler.

However, in the Viet Nam War, the left media exploited free speech to mislead the public by supporting Vietcong, which was an early terror organization in the Cold War. Actually, the left media companies in the US like *CNN, The Washington Post, The New York Times*, in Australia like *ABC, Channel Seven*, and the others plus the prominent leftists as Jane Fonda, John Kerry, Joe Biden, Bill and Hillary Clinton, and the Democratic high profiles officially endorsed Vietcong while the US soldiers were fighting against the Vietcong terrorist and the Global Communist Bloc in Viet Nam. The treasonous components in Viet Nam War still have enjoyed the free speech's deception, they have never shown the remorse by an apology to the millions of victims of Vietcong (Vietnamese people) and the US soldiers, allies (Viet Nam veteran).

Nowadays, the left media has exploited the free speech to endorse the terrorists in Western countries. Despite the government has no indictment of terrorism's supporters but the people recognize the domestic thug in mainstream media has propagated for terrorism. After the supreme leader of the Islamic State Abu Bakr al-Baghdadi exploded himself, the left media like *Channel Seven* in Australia broadcast the intimidation about the death of the Islamic State's leader sparks the terror while the Islamic State nearly disbanded. The people think the left media as *Channel Seven* represents Islamic State to appeal to the public by clever psychological warfare.

Recently, the death of two top terror generals of Iran that appeared the terror's endorsement in the West. In the US, Democrats outrage the deaths of two top terror commanders of Iran are military commander Abu Mahdi al-Huhamdis and Major General Qassem Soleimani who commander of the Islamic Revolution Guard Corps. The world welcomes two dangerous terrorists and the terror mastermind killed by the airstrike from the US's drone. Major General Qassem Soleimani plans to repeat the Benghazi's tragedy in Iraq by the attack the US embassy. In the passage of time, Major General Qassem Soleimani was the perpetrator of a terror in Washington, DC, in 2011, the target was a restaurant and Saudi Ambassador to the US, therefore, the first Muslim and communist President Barrack Obama did have the tough action when the terrorist attacked the people in the US soil.

The death of two top terror generals of Iran is also the woe of domestic thugs in the US. The Democratic Party slams President Donald Trump who ordered to kill two top terror commanders. It is not free speech while the country fights against terrorism and keeping the US safe. The highest profiles of Democrats are like Speak of House Nancy Pelosi who labels the airstrike is a disproportionate hit and conducts the war with Iran while the terrorist has not excepted any the targets including the Muslim countries (Indonesia, Pakistan, Iraq, and the others). Chairman of Intelligence Committee Adam Schiff and the Democratic lawmakers called the airstrike of President Donald Trump is reckless. Certainly, former Vice President Joe Biden attacks the airstrike of President Donald Trump, he said: "Trump just tossed a stick of dynamite into a tinderbox" and the presidential candidate Joe Biden hopes to us the US killed two top terror commanders to win the election in 2020. Therefore, after the airstrike, the approval rating of President Donald Trump skyrockets and it hit the highest record in three years. President Donald Trump twittered:

"Iran is talking very boldly about targeting certain USA assets as revenge for our ridding the world of their terrorist leader who had just killed an American and badly wounded many others, not to mention all of the people he had killed over his lifetime, including recently hundreds of Iranian protesters. He was already attacking our Embassy and preparing for additional hits in other locations. Iran has been nothing but problems for many years. Let this serves as a *warning* that if Iran strikes any Americans or American assets, we have targeted fifty-two Iranian sites (representing the fifty-two American hostages taken by Iran many years ago), some at a very high level & important to Iran & the Iranian culture, and those targets, and Iran itself, WILL BE HIT VERY FAST AND VERY HARD. The USA wants no more threats."

The *New York Times* exposes the terror's support, it is not the free speech when journalist Farnaz Fassihi criticizes the praise of the death of top terror commander Qassem Soleimani and this left journalist posted citing poetry of Soleimani. Certainly, the *New York Times* conceals the serious crimes of their icon Qassem Soleimani who supported the lethal assistance targeted to kill over six hundred Americans between 2003 to 2011. Instead, the *New York Times* praises the top commander of terror. The people can recognize the media companies threaten the terror escalates after the deaths of two top terror commanders, the left media use the free speech to appall the people and also support the rogue country into the psychological warfare.

The Muslims in London attended community memorial at the Islamic Center for the death of top terror commander Qassem Soleimani, the memorial service took twenty-five minutes. The United Kingdom fight against the terror, therefore, the Muslims adore the top terror commander. It is not freedom and free religious freedom, instead, the memorial to support terrorism. The UK intelligence may eye on Muslim communities, actually, after the death of two terror commanders are commander Abu Mahdi al-Huhamdis and Major General Qassem Soleimani. Two terror commanders and terror masterminds are important than Osama Bin Laden and Abu Bakr al-Baghdadi. Nevertheless, the United Kingdom is not Iran and Iraq.

In the US, the stronghold of Democrats, like Massachusetts, the terror's supporters protest against the anti-terrorism policy of the US government after two top terror commanders were killed, actually, the icon of terror's supporters is Major General Qassem Soleimani appearing in the logo of protestors. The United States of America is not Iran.

The death of two top terror generals appeared the domestic thugs in the West, the people and intelligence can recognize the terror's supporters in the US, UK, and other countries. The US and UK companies are scared to employ the terror's supporters, so the companies may lay off the dangerous workers that deal with national security.

China Crippled the Economic War with the US
By Hoa Truong
(Originally appeared on thedawnmedia.com on January 7, 2020)

The potential loss of China after the US tariffs struck right on the vulnerability of the largest communist country on the planet. The economic peril that dethroned the world's second-largest economy. Nowadays, China's communist regime faces the offshore market losses and the domestic problem when the export sector ruined that conducts massive jobless. The totalitarian regime being risked, so the communist knew their fate after more than seventy years ruled Chinese people by the terror methods, the demagogic policy carrying by propaganda and impoverished the people plus the obscurantism.

The character of the communist is heartless, the pupil of Marxism-Leninist-Maoist-Hồ Chí Minh thoughts have never respected the life of people, the social purge and socialism cause the death of more than 100 million people since the Lenin succeeded the Ape Revolution in October 1917. Moreover, the inhumane tactic or military genocide designed by Mao Tse Tung called" the human wave tactic" became the military disaster of the People's Liberation Army so, in the Korea War, Mao barbecued a million troops, untrained Four-Stars General Võ Nguyên Giáp exchanged the victory of Điện Biên Phủ's battle with ten thousands of Vietcong troops and North Viet Nam Communist claimed unpredictable victory with 1,500,000 lives of the People's Army of Viet Nam in the Viet Nam War. Therefore, the communist appalls the economic disaster and financial collapse.

The left media, the dishonest academics (the economic academics) crashed the credit after launching the phony psychological warfare to mislead the public, actually, the praise of China's economy and the trouble of the US economy by the retaliatory tariffs on China imposed the US agricultural products. Nowadays, the people have no trust the major fake news companies and also doubt the role of academics, they damaged the intellectual line by the lying reports, the biased documents to be debunked while the high technological communication and the multiple information sources plus the social media could testify a fake news or a fabricated story after released. Certainly, China couldn't conceal the potential loss after President Donald Trump launched the campaign to fight against the global economic terror that comes from China's communist regime. The so-called China dream that turned the nightmare when the economy crippled, the financial system is on the brink of collapse and currency devalued that surpassed the alert level.

The stock market represents the economic strength, unfortunately, in 2018, China's stock market worsened by the loss of $US 2.4 trillion or 25%, it is the biggest loss's record since China joined the free market and WTO. China grew from stolen technology and cunning business. China gained a profit from the malicious methods of the rogue country infiltrated into the international community. Therefore, China lost the major economic battles as a saying of Vietnamese" cut wood and stored for three years but burn down an hour." China surpassed the debt reached up to $US 40 trillion in 2017 or 300% GDP. Nowadays, the debt skyrockets after the US tariffs imposed and the giant telecommunication company Huawei is dead by the US banned and the world boycotted by the intelligence risk. China occupied 15% of world debt, the IMF warns the deep debt of China while the economy being aggravated. China's economic peril exposed in the mainland with more than 600 companies lost the stock market in 2018, the valuation evaporated 30% or $US 300 billion (3 trillion Yuan).

The loss of China could reflect the countries deeply involved with China from many decades ago. Australia is the victim of the trade trap, debt trap, and government trap when China's economy and finance tumbled, and Australia followed. In 2018, Australia paid the dire consequence after the critical mistake made in trade ties with China, the Australian Labor Party contributed to the disastrous economy and the naïve businesspersons collaborated with the rogue country. The short term's profit causes long-term damages, in 2018, the key benchmark ASX lost 7% or $AU 120 billion off the valuation of investors.

Europe faces the same situation, Germany's DAX, France's CAC 40 and the broad Euro Stoxx 50 lost more than 3%. Therefore, the US stabilized, the Dow Jones just fell under 2% and rebounded, in December 2019, Dow Jones reached 28,462 (Obama's era struggled under 17,000) and S & P 500 reached 3, 221. China reduces the aggressive attitude while facing the worst economy and financial trouble.

Almost, from the war fights against the global economic terror launched on July 6, 2018, China lost the major battles. The deep debt is the real threat, actually, the hegemonic ambition aggravated the financial burden on one belt and one road plus the cost to maintain the piratical stations into the disputed waters. Moreover, China also failed to use the Western's left media into propaganda while the tariffs imposing. The panic state of China reflects Democrats crazily impeach President Donald Trump and also China should incite Iran to provoke the US and conspiring to stray the US into military conflict. Actually, China will stay away if the US retaliates Iran, it is the malicious character of communist. Therefore, the US commander in chief advances the malicious plan by killing two top terror commanders of Iran. Certainly, Iran knows the Islamic Republic of Iran Army and the Revolutionary Guard Corps cannot confront with the strongest force on the planet, actually, the allies in the region as Saudi, Jordan, Israel can ruin Iran's army and if Iran attacks the US, NATO will involve. The intimidation of Iran's leaders reflects a saying" the barking dog never bites." actually, President Donald Trump warns the harsh retaliation will apply if Iran attacks the US. President Donald Trump twittered: "The United States just spent Two Trillion Dollars on Military Equipment. We are the biggest and by far the BEST in the World! If Iran attacks an American Base, or any American, we will be sending some of that brand-new beautiful equipment their way—and without hesitation!"

Democrats appear the treason and close friend with the rogue regime in Iran, the death of two top terror commanders that become the woe of Democratic Party, so the lawmaker terror leader Nancy Pelosi announces to limit President Donald Trump into taking military action against Iran.

Conclusion

After the Lê dynasty's rise and its quest to destroy the Mạcs, Mạc Văn Khiêm took the time to trace the family lineage as it fled from Hải Dương to the south through Bình Định, finally clearing the land and settling in Vĩnh Long Province.

I grew up in a Confucian family in Vĩnh Long Town and attended the West School. After Mạc Văn Nghĩa ran the West School, he became Governor Mission under Prime Minister Trần Văn Hửu. I attended Nguyễn Thông Public High School and went to Saigon after graduation to continue my education.

Like many young men in wartime, I joined the army in the 60s. During that time, I became a correspondent for *The Morning* newspaper with my contemporaries at other newspapers, Thái Dương and Nguyên Lương.

In the Year of the Monkey (1968), the VC did not keep its promise of a three-day ceasefire in South Viet Nam as people celebrated the start of spring. The North Viet Nam communists backed the VC attack on the cities and provincial capital of the RVN. Surprisingly, some of the provinces and cities were occupied by VC, but the South Vietnamese government managed to retake all but Huề and Quảng Trị, which were recaptured later.

I was injured when the VC attacked the province the second time on May 5, 1968, and received an honorable discharge from South Viet Nam's army. After April 30, 1975, along with military personnel, civil servants, and innocent civilians, I was imprisoned by the VC. They often used the term "reeducation" to describe our imprisonment. The "fake soldier, fake government" chased us into the New Economic Zone.

In 1980, I set sail across the sea in search of freedom, landing in Pulau Bidong, Malaysia. I served as the head of security there for a while, and then I left to settle in Pennsylvania in the United States. After that, I worked while going to school to earn enough money to be able to send for my family left behind in Viet Nam, and was fortunately able to eventually be reunited with them after many years of separation.

In 1992, under the pseudonym of Lê Trường Sơn, I founded *Rạng* Đông *Sunrise* magazine in Philadelphia. In 1996, I founded the Viet Nam Telephone Directory Company and published the commercial-services directory in the tri-state area of New York, New Jersey, and Pennsylvania, until it ceased publication in 2010. Although older, I am still active in my role as chairman of the board of the Vietnamese American Community of the United States (VACUSA), which lobbied Pennsylvania to recognize the flag of the Republic of Viet Nam in 2008.

In 2012, the City Council of Philadelphia approved allowing the VACUSA to raise the flag of the Republic of Viet Nam in the vestibule of Philadelphia City Hall each year from 9 a.m. to 5 p.m. on National Sorrow Day, April 30. In 2013, the Philadelphia Viet Nam Veterans Memorial Fund (PVVM) approved the construction of a Vietnamese American Memorial at Penn's Landing in South Philadelphia by the VACUSA. Construction began in 2014 and was completed in 2015.

In 1989, I met with the US Veterans Association, including Viet Nam veterans and ARVN veterans, at Cardinal Dougherty High School in North Philadelphia, establishing the Viet Nam Allied Veterans Association of Pennsylvania (VAVAP). The main purpose of the association is to build a US-Viet Nam memorial at the high school. The plan has the support of Reverend Paul Kennedy, principal of Cardinal Dougherty High School. Unfortunately, Reverend Kennedy and Richard Montgomery, president of the Allied Veterans, both fell seriously ill and died.

In 2011, I was invited by Frank "Bud" Kowalewski, a Viet Nam veteran, to a meeting of the Philadelphia Viet Nam Veterans Memorial Fund held at the administrative office of the VA. In the meeting, discussion was made of combining the restored American and Korean memorials into the Memorial Complex. Knowing this, I represented the CĐVNHK-VACUSA request to the PVVM council to approve building the Viet Nam-American Memorial in the area. After several meetings, the PVVM Association at last approved construction drawings for a Viet Nam flag alongside the US flag. In between the two flag poles is a granite wall that shows a brief-but-complete history of the Nationalist-Communist War in Viet Nam, including the five names of the South Vietnamese generals who committed suicide rather than surrender to the North Vietnamese. The restoration project and Memorial Park has the support of the city of Philadelphia, the US Veterans Association, and many US companies.

In 2019, The PVVM built a granite wall, but they failed to put the five names of the South Vietnamese generals as the PVVM promised: Aspirant General Trần Văn Hai (1925-1975), Aspirant General Lê Văn Hưng (1933-1975), Aspirant General Lê Nguyên Vỹ (1933-1975), Major General Nguyễn Khoa Nam (1927-1975), and Major General Phạm Văn Phú (1928-1975). The Board of Representatives of The Vietnamese American Community of the USA (VACUSA) has requested the PVVM reconsider putting the five Vietnamese generals on the granite wall as soon as possible. If they can't keep their promises, we can't support any projects raised by the PVVM.

QUANG HONG MAC (RAPHAEL M.V. MAC)

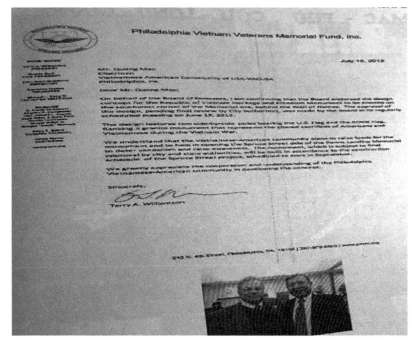

PVVM approved for VAC USA a land to build the
Vietnam Memorial at Penn's Landing on July 19, 2013

Appendix

Vietnamese American Community of USA- VACUSA

Non-Profit Organization, License number: 800598308
PO BOX 46754, Philadelphia, PA 19160 - Tel: 215-941-6484
Email: CDVNHK-VACUSA@yahoo.com

Announcement

Philadelphia, August 16, 2010

To: All Vietnamese refugees in the United States

Ref: Report of the Republic of Viet Nam flag to hang on the Ben
Franklin Parkway, Philadelphia Ladies and Gentlemen,

Mr. Quang Hong Mac, member of the Mayor's Commission
on Asian American Affairs, attended the meeting at 5:20 p.m.
on Monday, July 12, 2010, with Mr. Michael Nutter, mayor of
Philadelphia, regarding hanging the Republic of Viet Nam's flag
at Ben Franklin Parkway Boulevard. Because Mr. Quang Hong
Mac, Chairman, Board of Representatives of the Vietnamese
American Community of USA-VACUSA, disagreed with
the resolution of the City of Philadelphia in hanging flags of
both the Republic of Viet Nam and the Communist flag, Mr.
Anuj Gupta, chief of staff in the mayor's office, sent emails to
invite Mr. Quang Hong Mac, representing the Vietnamese
American Community in the United States, and Thoai Nguyen,

representing the SEAMAAC (Mutual Assistance Association Southeast Asian Coalition) to participate with city officials at 4:30 p.m. on Tuesday, July 20, 2010, in room 225 of City Hall.

In his email, Mr. Anuj Gupta said Quang Hong Mac may invite Vietnamese compatriots concerned about the flag of South Viet Nam and to let him know so that he could arrange the meeting. Realizing raising the South Vietnamese flag in the city of Philadelphia is a meaningful job and important for our Vietnamese refugees, we sent an email to all the leaders of the religious community, national associations, and fellow Viet Nam refugees that we had emails for. We needed to know the number of participants to let the city know. We first had ten people want to attend, but Mr. Gupta told Mr. Mac that due to the small meeting room only three could attend. However, Mr. Gupta had to move to room 221 to have enough seats. This session included:

1. Ms. Suzanne Biemiller, political advisor to the mayor (Presiding)
2. Mr. Anuj Gupta, mayor's chief of staff
3. Nina Ahmad, chair of the Advisory Committee for the mayor
4. Mr. Quang Hong Mac, Chairman of the Vietnamese American Community of USA- VACUSA
5. Mr. Frank "Bud" Kowalewski, Coordinator Allied Veterans Association of Pennsylvania
6. Mr. Loi Ma, employee of the City of Philadelphia
7. Mr. Stanley Nguyen, a member of the Federation of Vietnamese American Voters Pennsylvania
8. Mr. Thoai Nguyen, representing the SEAMAAC (nonprofit charities founded by Mr. Dick Wenner in the 80s), Fellowship Commission, and the Assembly

of Viet Nam, China, Cambodia, Laos, and Hmong. Currently, five members—Viet Nam, Cambodia, Laos, Hmong, and China have pulled out of the SEAMAAC Assembly, but still work under the name of SEAMAAC with new members.

9. A cadet from West Point, second boarding intern for the chief of staff.

The meeting began with an introduction by Mr. Anuj Gupta. Mr. Gupta said that the meeting was to solve the issue with Viet Nam flag at Ben Franklin Parkway Blvd., that in its meeting on July 20, 2010, Mr. Quang Hong Mac did not agree with the proposal to hang both the South Vietnamese flag and the Communist flag. Therefore, Mr. Gupta wanted to know the decision of the Vietnamese Community of how to work the Vietnamese flag in during the coming September.

Mr. Quang Hong Mac answered clearly and decisively that the Vietnamese refugee community in Philadelphia, as well those across the United States, will not accept the Communist flag. Mr. Quang Hong Mac also cited cases related by Tran Truong in California where fifty thousand Vietnamese refugees protested for 55 days and nights before his shop because of the display of the flag and a picture of communist Ho Chi Minh. The city of Los Angeles was the first city in the United States to already have legislation preventing the Communist delegation in the city because of security concerns.

Next, Mr. Thoai Nguyen, representing the SEAMAAC Assembly, stated that despite growing up in the United States, he had visited Viet Nam several times. He saw Viet Nam changed and developed. He also said that his father was a former soldier who stayed in Viet Nam, and he agreed with hanging flags of both the Republic of Viet Nam and Communist Viet Nam.

Mr. Quang Hong Mac asked Frank "Bud" Kowalewski for comments. Kowalewski saw combat in Viet Nam in 1967-1968 and was wounded and honorably discharged. He is now coaching for a school in New Jersey. He said that the South Vietnamese flag should hang on Ben Franklin Parkway Blvd. because the yellow flag with three red stripes symbolizes the Republic of Viet Nam and the traditional freedom of Vietnamese refugees in Philadelphia.

Nina Ahmad said the South Vietnamese flag was no longer recognized by the United Nations, and Mr. Gupta followed that if the South Vietnamese flag was flown without the Communist flag, the Communist embassy would protest. Mr. Gupta asked Mr. Quang Hong Mac if he wanted only the flag of South Viet Nam to fly no matter if the Communist embassy objected. Mr. Quang replied that the Communist protest is their right, but the city is also right to fly the flag of the Republic of Viet Nam. For example, in the city of Los Angeles, even though the Communist embassy protested, the mayor still signed a law banning the Communist delegation to the city for failing to ensure security for them.

Mrs. Nina Ahmad said it was in California and not in Philadelphia. Mr. Stanley Nguyen and Mr. Loi Ma backed Mr. Mac's stance and disagreed with hanging the SRV flag.

Mr. Gupta added the second solution was that if the Vietnamese refugee community did not want to fly the flag with the Communist flag, the flag of South Viet Nam could fly at the Viet Nam Memorial in Penn's Landing along Columbus Blvd. and the Communist flag at Ben Franklin.

This second solution was not agreed to by the Vietnamese delegation, and the meeting ended without any final resolution of the South Vietnamese flag at Ben Franklin Parkway as Mayor Michael Nutter had promised the Vietnamese who supported him before the election.

As a voice of Vietnamese Americans and fellow Viet Nam refugees in Philadelphia and the vicinity who have to pay taxes and vote, we have consulted with the elders and other notables and sent a letter to Michael Nutter, mayor of Philadelphia, through email to Anuj Gupta.

Mr. Gupta then sent an email to Mr. Quang and said that he had received many of the Vietnamese petitions addressed to the mayor and said he is not hanging the Republic of Viet Nam and the Communist flag together in September this year.

Respectfully,
Quang Hong Mac
Chairman, Vietnamese American
Community of USA-VACUSA

Commissioner, Mayor's Commission on Asian American Affairs for Michael Nutter, Mayor of Philadelphia

Chairman, Asian American and Pacific Advisory Committee for Tom Corbett, the Attorney General of Pennsylvania.

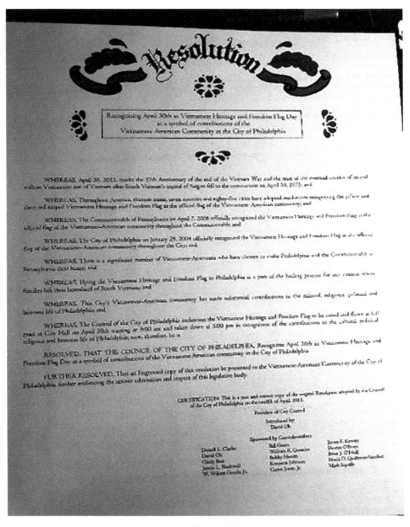

Councilman At-Large David Oh (R) presents the resolution to the VACUSA on April 12, 2012, to hang the Republic of Viet Nam flag at the front of the City Hall in Philadelphia from 9 a.m. to 5 p.m. each year.

Hon. Dennis M. O'Brien (R) Speaker of the House (PA),
signed HR-613 on April 7, 2008, to recognize
the RVN flag as a Vietnamese heritage and freedom flag.
On Monday April 30, 2012, the VACUSA organized honoring
the RVN flag in South Philadelphia.

The Former South Vietnam Army Association
celebrated after receiving the HR. 613 in 2008

List of Vietnamese Family Names

by Late Professor Huy Ngọc Nguyen who has given an original
to Le Truong Son in 1999

1.An	2.Ân	3.Ất	4.Âu	5. Âu Dương	6.Bá
7.Bạch	8.Bàn	9.Bàng	10.Bành	11.Bao	12.Bảo
13. Bát	14.Bạt	15. Bật	16. Bề	17. Bì	18. Biên
19. Biện	20. Binh	21. Bồ	22. Bộ	23. Bốc	24. Bùi
25. Cá	26. Cái	27. Cam	28. Cao	29. Cáp	30. Cát
31. Cầm	32.Cấn	33.Cấp	34.Cố	35.Cồ	36. Cổ
37. Cốc	38. Công	39. Cơ	40. Cù	41. Cung	42. Chàm
43. Chàng	44. Châu	45. Chề	46. Chi	47. Chiêm	48. Chu
49. Chúc	50. Chung	51. Chử	52. Chức	53. Chương	54. Danh
55. Dân	56. Diệp	57. Diên	58. Diệu	59. Doãn	60. Du
61. Duy	62. Dư	63. Dương	64. Dữu	65. Đa	66. Đái
67. Đam	68. Đàm	69. Đan	70. Đàn	71. Đào	72. Đắc

73. Đằng	74. Đặng	75. Đâu	76. Đèo	77. Địch	78. Điểm
79. Điến	80. Điệp	81. Điêu	82. Điệu	83. Đinh	84. Đoàn
85. Đòi	86. Đô	87. Đỗ	88. Đồng	89. Đổng	90. Đới
91. Đơn	92. Đức	93. Đường	94. Gia Các	95. Gia Cát	96. Giả
97. Giải	98. Giang	99. Giao	100. Giáp	101 Giẹp	102. Giệp
103. Hà	104. Hạ	105. Hạ Hầu	106. Hai	107. Hán	108. Hàn
109. Hàng	110. Hạp	111. Hấn	112. Hầu	113. Hi	114. Hình
115. Hoa	116. Hoan	117. Hoàn	118. Hoàng	119. Hoàng Phủ	120. Hoắc
121. Hồ	122. Hồi	123. Hồng	124. Huê	125. Hung	126. Hùng
127. Huy	128. Huỳnh	129. Hứa	130. Hữu	131. Ích	132. Kiển
133. Kiều	134. Kiểu	135. Kim	136. Kính	137. Kỳ	138. Kha
139. Khang	140. Khâu	141. Khiều	142. Khoa	143. Khổng	144. Khuất
145. Khúc	146. Khương	147. Khưu	148. La	149. Lã	150. Lạc
151. Lai	152. Lại	153. Lan	154. Lang	155. Lãnh	156. Lao
157. Lão	158. Lâm	159. Lê	160. Lếu	161. Liêm	162. Liên
163. Liêng	164. Liêu	165. Liễu	166. Linh	167. Liu	168. Loan
169. Long	170. Lô	171. Lồ	172. Lỗ	173. Lộ	174. Lộc
175. Lục	176. Luyện	177. Lũ	178. Lữ	179. Lương	180. Lưu
181. Lý	182. Ma	183. Mã	184. Mạc	185. Mạch	186. Mai
187. Man	188. Mạnh	189. Mao	190. Mẫn	191. Mân	192. Mịch
193. Mộ Dung	194. Mục	195. Mui	196. Nam	197. Ninh	198. Nông
199. Nồng	200. Nùng	201. Nfạc	202. Nfạn	203. Nghê	204. Nghi
205. Nghĩa	206. Nghiêm	207. Nghiên	208. Ngọc	209. Ngô	210. Ngu
211. Ngũ	212. Nguơn	213. Nguy	214. Nguyên	215. Nguyễn	216. Ngưu
217. Nhạc	218. Nhan	219. Nhâm	220. Nhậm	221. Nhân	222. Nhữ
223. Oác	224. Ô	225. Ôn	226. Ông	227. Phác	228. Phạm
229. Phán	230. Phàn	231. Phàng	232. Phi	233. Phí	234. Phó
235. Phò	236. Phòng	237. Phú	238. Phù	239. Phụ	240. Phúc
241. Phục	242. Phùng	243. Phương	244. Quách	245. Quan	246. Quản
247. Quang	248. Quất	249. Quề	250. Quyên	251. Roãn	252. Sa

93

253. Sái	254. Sài	255. Sam	256. Sầm	257. Sĩ	258. Soán
259. Sở	260. Son	261. Sùng	262. Sư	263. Sử	264. Sương
265. Tả	266. Tạ	267. Tào	268. Tăng	269. Tân	270. Tấn
271. Tần	272. Tập	273. Tất	274. Tích	275. Tiền	276. Tiến
277. Tiết	278. Tiêu	279. Tinh	280. Toàn	281. Tô	282. Tôn
283. Tôn Thất	284. Tông	285. Tống	286. Tu	287. Tú	288. Tuấn
289. Tư Mã	290. Từ	291. Tưởng	292. Thạch	293. Thái	294. Thang
295. Thành	296. Thẩm	297. Thân	298. Thê	299. Thi	300. Thích
301. Thiếu	302. Thiện	303. Thinh	304. Thoại	305. Thoán	306. Thôi
307. Thông	308. Thượng	309. Trà	310. Trác	311. Trang	312. Trần
313. Trân	314. Trí	315. Trích	316 Triều	317. Triệu	318. Trình
319. Trịnh	320. Trọng	321. Trưng	322. Trương	323. Ủ	324. Uất
325. Ung	326. Uông	327. Ứng	328. Vạn	329. Văn	330. Vân
331. Vệ	332. Vi	333. Viêm	334. Viện	335. Việt	336. Vinh
337. Võ	338. Vòng	339. Vũ	340. Vương	341. Vưu	342. Wòng
343. Xa	344. Xuân	345. Xung	346. Xử	347. Yên	348. Yêu

Note: There are 348 Vietnamese family names dating back four thousand years.

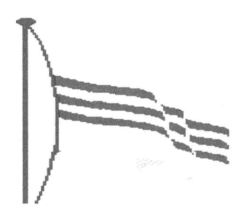

Artwork of Viet Nam flag

The National Flag of Free Viet Nam

Exiled Vietnamese around the world only recognize the yellow flag with three red stripes.

Quốc-Ca Việt-Nam Cộng-Hòa (National Anthem of Free Viet Nam)

> Này công-dân ơi! Đứng lên đáp lời sông-núi!
> Đồng lòng cùng đi, hy-sinh tiếc gì thân sống.
> Vì tương-lai quốc-dân, cùng xông-pha khói tên,
> Làm sao cho núi sông từ nay luôn vững bến.
> Dù cho thây phơi trên gươm-giáo,
> Thù nước lấy máu đào đem báo!
> Nòi-giống lúc biến phải cần giải nguy,
> Người công-dân luôn vững-bến tâm-trí,
> Hùng-tráng quyết chiến-đấu làm cho khắp nơi,
> Vang tiếng người Nước-Nam cho đền muôn đời.
> Công-dân ơi! Mau hiến-thân dưới cờ!
> Công-dân ơi! Mau làm cho cõi-bờ,
> Thoát cơn tàn-phá, vẻ-vang nòi-giống,
> Xứng danh nghìn năm dòng-giống Lạc-Hồng.*

Ghi-Chú (Notes): "Lạc-Hồng" hay "Hồng-Lạc": các vị vua đầu-tiên của dân Việt, Vua Hồng-Bàng (King-Dương-Vương) và Lạc-Long-Quân. Trong triều-đại đầu-tiên của dân Việt (2879-258 trước tây-lịch), Kinh Dương Vương (Hồng-Bàng) là vị vua đầu-tiên của nước ta, Lạc-Long-Quân là vị vua thứ nhì của nước ta.

National Anthem of the Republic of Viet Nam
(English translation by Khai-Chinh Pham Kim-Thu)

> Oh, citizens! Stand up to respond to the fatherland's request!
> With the same heart we go, sacrifice ourselves, don't
> regret our lives.

For our people's future, together we enter the warfare
with courage!

Try to secure our fatherland to be always durable from
now on!

Even if our corpses display on weapons,

For national revenge, we should take our rosy blood to
avenge!

When our race has calamity, we must deliver our people
from danger!

Citizens should always be stable in mind!

Determine mightily to struggle everywhere,

To make Vietnamese reputation resound forever!

Oh, citizens! Hurry up to offer your lives under the
national flag!

Oh, citizens! Hurry up to help our fatherland

Escape from destruction, make our race glorious,

To be eternally worthy of the Lac-Hong race![1]

US Cities and States Recognize the Free Vietnamese Flag

On February 19, 2003, from the city of Westminster, California, bypassing the states in alphabetical order: Colorado, Florida, Georgia, Hawaii, Indiana, Kansas, Louisiana, Massachusetts, Mississippi, Michigan, Minnesota, Nebraska, New York, New Jersey, Oklahoma, Oregon, Pennsylvania, Texas, Utah, Virginia, and Washington. To November 7, 2004, the Viet Nam national flag, with three red stripes on a yellow background, was formally recognized in the following chronological order:

---

1   "Lac-Hong" or "Hong-Lac" are the ancestors of the Vietnamese race, Hong-Bang (Kinh-Duong-Vuong) and Lac-Long-Quan. In the first dynasty in Vietnamese history (2879-258 BC), Hong-Bang (King Duong Vuong) is the first king of Viet Nam, while Lac-Long-Quan is the second.

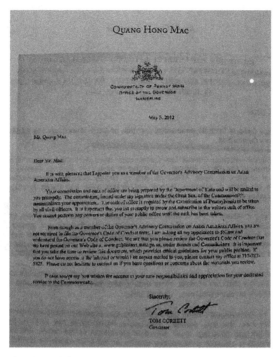

- Hon. Tom Corbett, PA governor appointed Mr. Quang Mac as a member of The Governor's Advisory Commission in Asian American Affairs.

Marlene R. Moster, MD
12-10-2019

To Mr. Mac

It is people like you that make the world turn! Due to your ethics, superior conduct, and deep feeling for others, you make the world a better place.

With deep respect,
Marlene R. Moster. MD

Professor of Ophthalmology, Thomas Jefferson School of Medicine Wills Eye Hospital

MARLENE R. MOSTER MD

Drs. Chuong Trinh and Phuong Trinh
12-11-2019

Mr. Mac is an authority on Vietnamese affairs. This book uses plain wording and varied resources to make it easier for the user to understand the content. It is important for people to introduce the book's research strategy to the young Vietnamese generation to help them understand more about the Viet Nam War.

Best regards,
Chuong Trinh MD and
Phuong Trinh MD

Chuong Trinh MD and Phuong Trinh MD

Duc Mac's Family

Tri Mac's Family

Lan anh Mac's Family

Lan chi Mac's Family

Quang Mac's Family

VAC USA & PPAAAC activities
PPAAAC Holiday Party 2019

Mr. Quang Mac presented a book to
Dr. Dawn Salvatore (Jefferson Hospital)

A picture of Vietnamese Abroad
Pen Center

Mr. Quang Mac with Viet nam Veterans

PPAAAC Holiday Party 2015

Picture of Hong Mac, Duy Mac, Quyen Le, and Quang Mac

Mr. and Mrs. Mac's 50ᵗʰ anniversary with (L-R) Mr & Mrs. Dong Nguyen; Msgr. Joseph Trinh; Mr. & Mrs Raphael Mac; Chief Inspector Cynthia Dorsey and Peter Mac .

Hong Mac with his wife Minh Pham and Duy Mac with his son Tyler Mac

Chianna Mac and Sarah Barden on a trip in South Korea

Review Requested:

We'd like to know if you enjoyed the book.
Please consider leaving a review on the platform
from which you purchased the book.

CPSIA information can be obtained
at www.ICGtesting.com
Printed in the USA
LVHW080801310720
661936LV00009B/1191